A **WAR**
We Must
WIN

A WAR
We Must
WIN

A Frontline Account of the Battle Against the Pornography Conspiracy

John Harmer

Bookcraft
Salt Lake City, Utah

Library of Congress Catalog Card Number: 99-72526

ISBN 1-57008-649-4

First Printing, 1999

Printed in the United States of America

To the memory of Kelly Hulme
"Lest we forget, lest we forget"
and
To Jim Clancy and Ernie Schulzke—
Two men who are totally without guile.

CONTENTS

INTRODUCTION

On the morning of Wednesday, November 28, 1973, when I was in my office at the state capitol in Sacramento, California, my secretary told me that Russell Hulme, a stake president in Saratoga, California, was on the phone. Russell's brother, Bishop Paul Hulme, had been a loyal friend of mine since our days as students at the University of Utah. When I picked up the phone Russell's voice was grave and emotional.

"Are you aware of what happened yesterday?" he asked.

"No. What's wrong?"

President Hulme then went on to inform me that on the previous afternoon Paul's ten-year-old daughter, Kelly, had been brutally sexually abused and then murdered while on her way home from school. The details were still confused, and the police were still proceeding with an investigation. Somehow Kelly had been lured into an abandoned house located in an orchard through which she would take a shortcut to get home. In that house she had been viciously tortured and then murdered. Several hours after her parents had notified the police she was missing, her mutilated body was found in the garage of the house.

"Paul and Helga would like you to speak at the funeral. Can you make it?"

While I was still dealing with the stunning reality of what he was saying I made arrangements to be at the funeral. Several months earlier I had spoken at a fireside in the chapel of the ward where Kelly's father was the bishop. As part of the program that evening, Kelly and her two sisters, as a trio, had sung several songs. I rcmembered watching her radiant expression, the delightful enthusiasm of her countenance as she sang, her blond hair giving the appearance of a halo about her head and setting off her pink cheeks. Now she was dead, the victim of a vicious and hideously brutal crime.

Eventually the guilty party was found. He was a nineteen-year-old man who lived near the home of Paul and Helga Hulme. In his room at his home was a supply of vile pornographic literature. One of these publications outlined in sordid detail the sadomasochistic torture that had been inflicted on little Kelly Hulme. In the end his crazed sexual madness resulted in her death.

The pathos of this scenario was that Paul Hulme had been one of the most effective and involved citizen volunteers in my efforts to secure the passage of a statewide ballot initiative dealing with the production and distribution of pornographic literature and motion pictures. In what was more than just a supreme irony, and one of the most cruel of all possible scenarios, his own daughter was the victim of the very evil we were working so hard to eliminate.

It is well documented that in the United States during the past forty years there have been not just hundreds but literally thousands of innocent victims of the pornographers, their suffering and death being similar to that of Kelly Hulme. In the pages that follow I outline the combinations of evil and conspiring men and women who produce and distribute this degenerate material, and how they have with lies and distortions been able to deny their guilt.

Why have I written this book? Having watched the evolution of the nature of pornographic materials in our society for the past thirty years, and having been correct in my prior predictions as to what would happen if we failed to take action (we did fail and it did happen), I feel compelled this one last time to raise a voice of warning.

Though I make the comment respectfully, it is also with some dismay that I make reference to the tremendous naiveté of most Latter-day Saint parents and priesthood leaders with regard to the incredible volume of pornography in American society in general and among Latter-day Saint youth in particular. The annual dollar

volume in pornography makes the conclusion undeniable that this
plague of sleaze permeates every community, every neighborhood,
and, tragically, many homes in which families are being destroyed by
its poison. Consider the following:

— In 1996 the rentals and sales of pornographic videos made up
  more than 13 percent (13.1%) of the entire videocassette
  market, with sales revenue of $4 billion.
— In videocassette rental and sales stores that carry both general release films and pornography, the pornography sales
  and rentals were nearly 28 percent (27.8%) of the total.
— In hard numbers, during 1996, stores in the United States
  reported a total of 665 million rentals of pornographic videocassettes.
— The single largest segment of Internet commerce is "on-line
  adult services" (meaning pornography), with over $1 billion
  in annual subscriber fees.

We have now come to a point where the technology of electronic
communications can bring the most degenerate visual and verbal filth
directly to the home. It can be seen on the TV set in the family den
or on the computer monitor screen in the study, or heard on the CD
player in the bedroom. The pornographers have achieved their goals.
They have found the way to market directly into the home; they have
made pornography acceptable to women; and they have been able to
seduce younger and younger people into the web of pornography,
thus vastly increasing present and future profits. These profits are
huge, and indeed are the driving force for the production and distribution of pornography throughout the world.

The massive financial power of the pornography industry and
their accomplices in the Motion Picture Association of America
(MPAA), the slick magazine publishers, and the Recording Industry
of America (RIAA) have completely dominated the agenda in state
legislatures and the national Congress as regards any anti-pornography efforts. With their funding of the American Civil Liberties
Union (ACLU) this secret combination of Satan's workers are now
poised to unleash a time of public carnality and adulation of sensuous
behavior that has never existed since the fall of Adam. With arrogance and with a success that is as numbing as the bite of a poisonous

serpent, they have brought pornography from the sewer to the highest levels of academic prominence.

Our youth need to know how pornography is created and distributed by organized crime, the motion picture industry, the slick magazine publishers, and the myriad neurotic exhibitionists who have found an outlet for their sick minds through the Internet.

My fear is that through many years of imperceptible compromise the Latter-day Saints have become so desensitized to that which they should abhor that they now cannot clearly discern evil when it comes before them. I find presumably faithful Latter-day Saints recommending with approval motion pictures, books, magazines, and stage plays whose messages are anything but "virtuous, lovely, of good report, or praiseworthy." Thus we accept without protest the presence in our midst of conduct and entertainment that thirty years ago would have generated a storm of indignation. If this does not represent an erosion of our core values, how else can we explain it?

Awakening the Latter-day Saints to that reality is why this book may be of value. One of the first rules of success in any war is to "know thine enemy." The pornographers are indeed one of the secret combinations of evil which Moroni prophesied would be extant in the last days (see Ether 8:21–25). The purpose of this book is to enable parents, teachers, and yes, the addicted victim of pornography, to understand how radically evil this pernicious material really is, and what must be the ultimate destiny of an individual or a society that embraces it.

I referred above to the pornography addict. In Chapter 12 I review my own experience of becoming conscious of the loss of light and the Spirit of the Lord in my life as I was required to see and hear the most depraved forms of pornographic material. The sacred and deeply personal experience that I have shared there convinces me that anyone who truly desires to be "cleansed" from the horrible soul-staining effect of pornography can realize their desire. It is neither easy nor pleasant, but the "iron furnace" of fasting, prayer, and other spiritual exercises can purge away the memory and the effect of the vile material. The certainty of these truths is why I have written what I have written.

PART ONE

THE
PROBLEM

———————

CHAPTER ONE

IN SUN VALLEY:
THE END OF INNOCENCE

In the spring of 1964 I was a young attorney practicing law in Glendale, California. Some weeks earlier I had prepared for one of my clients a lease on certain warehouse space located farther out in the San Fernando Valley in an area referred to as "Sun Valley." The lease having been executed and the appropriate rent paid, the matter was soon forgotten as I proceeded with other issues.

That obscure lease of a small warehouse in Los Angeles County was to have a profound impact on the direction of my life. The tenant was a major distributor of pornographic magazines.

The Los Angeles district attorney's office had traced the distribution of a new group of pornographic magazines back to my client's warehouse. A very anxious client had called me to come to his office and explain the circumstances to one James Clancy, a deputy district attorney assigned to the prosecution of distributors and marketers of pornographic material.

Clancy was a classic example of the proverbial "bantam rooster." Though small, he was so tenacious and so persevering that he would fearlessly take on much larger and stronger foes. While in size he was small, for courage, moral integrity, and tenacity of commitment I have never met a greater man. The day we first met at my client's warehouse was to begin a lifelong friendship of cooperation and frustration in the battle against the pornography industry.

After I was able to demonstrate my client's innocence as to the contents of the warehouse, we began the process that I assumed would put the distributor out of business. I soon learned how naive I was in thinking that closing up one distribution location or confiscating the contraband materials would impede the activities of even a minor player in the vast network of the pornography industry.

At Clancy's request I participated in the ensuing attempt to prosecute the distributor. That was when I had my first contact with the attorneys who defend these people, and with their very active co-conspirators, the American Civil Liberties Union (ACLU). Though we had what I was confident was irrefutable evidence, the statutory authority, and the proof of violation of the law, the defendant was not even briefly interrupted in the process of distributing what was then deemed to be "hard-core" pornography. That was the first of what were to be dozens of similar experiences in which notwithstanding the clear intent of the law, the grossness of the violation, and the certainty of the evidence, the pornographer would walk out of court without any penalty, or at most a minor inconvenience in the form of a small fine. Before I was back at my office in Glendale the pornographer was back in business.

The contents of that warehouse in Sun Valley, Los Angeles County, California, were the first pornographic material I had ever seen. In 1964, this material the D.A. had confiscated would be rated at about an 85 on a scale of one to a hundred. In other words, in severity of content, in its graphic portrayal of perversion, it was considered to be close to the ultimate extreme of what was then being produced.

Some thirty years later that same material, on the same scale of one to a hundred, would be rated at about 15. In other words, in that thirty-year period the nature of the material being produced and distributed in the dark world of pornography would have moved so much farther into the realm of depravity and vileness that what in 1964 was close to the extreme was now among the very tamest of material that would be considered pornography. As the American culture had become increasingly desensitized to this material, the producers had to become more and more extreme in what they graphically depicted in print and on film and videotape.

How amazingly brutalized our culture has become was illustrated in an article printed in the *Wall Street Journal* of Tuesday, May

5, 1998. The article, by Roger Kimball, was entitled, "What Next, a Doctorate of Depravity?" The intent of the article was to recite the bizarre emergence upon university and college campuses of conferences and courses of study on "depravity," presented primarily by exhibitionist academics who had no other way to distinguish themselves. In referring to one of these conferences the author noted: "With some dozen papers on subjects like 'Sodomy, Miscegenation, and the Impossibility of Privacy,' and 'Queer Politics as Vocation: Sexuality and the Package Deal of Multiculturalism' the author provided a vivid taste of what passes these days for instruction in the humanities and social sciences. Only a few years ago, so-called queer theory occupied a place on the fringes of academic respectability. Today it is one of the trendiest academic fiefdoms in the humanities, the occasion for myriad classes, conferences, articles, journals and books. Harvard, Stanford, Duke, Columbia and the University of California at Berkeley were among the most prestigious institutions represented at 'Queer Publics/Queer Privates.' "

In this same article the author quotes one of the academic participants in the so-called conference who illustrated how quickly our culture comes to accept the unacceptable. "B. Ruby Rich from U.C. Berkeley pursued a variation on this theme: 'Back in the '80s when butch-femme was transgressive,' she said, many students in one of her classes were disconcerted by the 'extreme sadomasochism' of a film she screened. Just last week, though, 'it wasn't even recognized as such by students of today'—a development, she rightly observed, that showed 'how quickly transgression becomes invisible.' "

There you have it. In the 1980s a pornographic film depicting sadomasochistic behavior (i.e., sexually oriented torture or sadistic abuse of another) was shown to a group of students who expressed "concern" at the nature of the conduct in the film, which involved sadistic abuse or torture of another. By 1998, when the same film was shown to a current group of students, not only was there no objection to the sadomasochistic conduct in the film, but *the audience did not even recognize it as such!*

In 1964 sadomasochism had just begun to appear in the mainstream of pornographic materials, and by today's standards would have been considered mild. By the early seventies, when Kelly

Hulme was the victim of a sadomasochistic torture and murder, it had become much more evident but was still considered on the outer fringe of pornography. Today the depictions of sadomasochism have moved to the extreme of what in the industry are referred to as "snuff films," where the victim of the sadomasochistic sexual abuse is literally and actually murdered in front of the camera. This is how far we have gone in less than one generation of pornographic depiction.

I first learned of "snuff" films from an FBI agent in 1971. After that time I came across the producers and sellers of "snuff" films on several occasions. Even the ultra-liberal minds at the ACLU have not seen fit to come forth and attempt to defend these perversions, which descend to a depth of depravity that defies human comprehension. Yet it must not be forgotten that these films exist because there is a demand for them from individuals whose addiction to pornography has now become so obsessive that the only way they could be satisfied in their craving for erotica was to see the actual torture and murder of a young girl recorded on film.

The FBI tell me that a true "snuff" film on videocassette can command as much as $500. Following are two brief descriptions of how the makers of "snuff" films seduce young girls into their clutches.

STOCKTON—A convicted child molester appeared in San Joaquin County Superior Court Thursday to be arraigned on charges of attempting to kidnap a young girl and make her his sex slave before videotaping her murder as part of a "snuff" film. Harold Wayne Tomason, 46, is named in an 11-count criminal complaint charging him with solicitation to commit kidnaping, murder, sodomy and rape. . . . An undercover police officer was initially investigating an alleged attempt to buy pornographic magazines involving children, Sgt. Tom Morris said. But Morris said the seriousness of the case suddenly escalated when the officer was asked to kidnap a blond girl about 8 years old whom Tomason had seen unsupervised outside a duplex in north Stockton. Tomason, who has a child molestation conviction in Oregon, wanted to use a stun gun to capture the girl, then tie her up and drive her to a cabin he planned to rent near Fresno, Morris said. "He was going to perform sex with her for about 30 days, train her to be his sex slave," Morris added. "*After he got done with her, he wanted to film her death, which in those circles is referred to as a snuff film."* (*The Modesto Bee,* November 11, 1991; emphasis added.)

The following article involves a similar but much more sophisticated "snuff" film maker who operated out of his home in West Caldwell, New Jersey.

A New Jersey video producer who admitted operating a child pornography business from his West Caldwell home was sentenced yesterday to 12½ years in prison by a federal judge who revealed U.S. authorities had uncovered evidence linking the defendant to the planning of "snuff" films.

Authorities disclosed that the FBI was able to obtain tape recording in which the suspect, Louis Ferriol, 45, was heard discussing the proposed abduction, torture and murder of a young child.

A source said government investigators believe that Ferriol, . . . could help expose details of the underground child porn and "snuff" film industry.

. . . U.S. District Judge Maryanne Trup Barry charged that Ferriol . . . had been involved in the distribution of violent sex films and child pornography for years. Barry said evidence revealed, however, that his "thirst for violence" had grown to the point where he was actively involved in the planning of a "snuff" movie involving the murder of a child.

"Snuff" films were described by one federal official as underground movies in which anonymous victims are graphically tortured and murdered on camera in bizarre sexual rituals. Some investigators believe that many disappearances in remote parts of the U.S. may be linked to the production of such films.

Tape recordings obtained by the FBI, Barry said, revealed Ferriol discussing the gruesome details of the kidnap and torture-murder of children. (Robert Rudolph, *The Star-Ledger,* July 31, 1991.)

Because the existence of the "snuff" film is the actual evidence of a murder, the traffic in these films is obviously very tightly supervised among the pornographers and their clients. The high cost of owning a "snuff" film, along with the liability, restricts the traffic in them to only the most addicted pedophiles. But the demand is there and the films exist and are continuing to be produced. It is my personal experience that those who ultimately seek out the "snuff" film began their descent into the abyss of pornography with the same "harmless" erotica that is so feverishly defended by the ACLU and the attorneys who make their living defending the pornography industry.

One of the many lessons I first learned in that experience in Sun Valley is that pornography has no shelf life; it never becomes obsolete. The only pornographers who have a problem with "dated" material are the publishers of the various slick magazines that are commonly sold from magazine racks in airports, convenience stores, and hotel gift shops. Most pornographic material never carries a publication date, because it can be sold for years after it is originally printed or filmed and still be acceptable to the purchaser. In Sun Valley we destroyed over ten thousand individual magazines stored in that warehouse. Confident that we had made a major impact on the vultures who ply this trade, I later learned that the loss of ten thousand of their magazines was such a minor inconvenience that it took only hours to replace the inventory at another location.

Such was my naiveté. Equally naive was my assumption that the end of the saga in Sun Valley would be my last contact with the world of depravity.

Pornographers thrive for two basic reasons: first, the immense profits that accrue from the production and distribution of their vile materials; second, the seemingly insatiable curiosity so many of the human race have for the bizarre, the obscene, and the depraved. It is tragic but true that curiosity becomes an appetite and then an addiction. But for the addiction to be satisfied, the grossness of the depravity has to become more and more extreme. That is why over the years in which I have been something of a participant in this arena I have seen the grossness of the material being produced and distributed extend to greater and greater extremes.

I am not a clinical psychologist and do not presume to make further comment on the nature of mankind's susceptibility to the obscene. For whatever reason, filth and vice are much more compelling to much of mankind than are virtue and decency. I leave it to such authorities as Dr. Victor Cline to explain that aspect of the existence of pornography among us. As to the more obvious factor, and

the principal motivator for the pornographers—the profits involved—
I can speak with some authority based on direct experience. Pornography makes huge profits. At one time it was dominated by the organized crime families of America, but the evolution of technology that has made the production and distribution of pornography so much easier has taken away the power of organized crime syndicates to control the distribution channels. The vast expansion of the market for pornography has also prevented any particular group from controlling the distribution process.

As noted earlier, this book is not intended to be either a legal treatise on the law of obscenity or an effort to analyze the powerful addictive enticement of pornography. What this book is intended to accomplish is to enlighten the reader with an understanding of the incredible spread of this plague throughout our society and the ultimate demise of any culture that long tolerates its presence.

Pornography has now become accepted and distributed on a scale so huge that to describe its size and depth it can only be likened to a tidal wave. I have watched this black plague of filth produce on our society the burden of disease and personal and family tragedy. During that time the pornographers have grown in power and arrogance as their willing accomplices, the motion picture industry and the slick magazine publishers, have participated in the slow but constant erosion of the values and the moral sensitivity of our society.

As pornography has increased in presence and volume it has continued to become more and more degenerate. All the while the monetary profits to the pornographers have continued to roll in.

Let me give one illustration of how profitable pornography can be. In the mid-1960s a most vile pornographic motion picture was produced called *Deep Throat.* The total production cost was less than one hundred thousand dollars. Whenever in any given community it was prosecuted for exhibition and distribution, without exception it was judged to be hard-core pornography. Notwithstanding that, over a period of nearly twenty years of widespread distribution in adult theaters, and later in the sale of videocassettes, the film generated revenue of over forty-five million dollars, a return of more than four hundred twenty-five dollars for every dollar invested. Such is the incentive for the producers of depravity.

Because I was willing to take the time away from my law practice and to risk the contempt of the media for my efforts, Jim Clancy came back to me on a variety of occasions to assist him in his struggle to stem the production and exhibition of pornographic materials in Los Angeles County. A devout Roman Catholic and a fearless crusader, Clancy was deeply committed to the protection of the community from the insidious effects of sexually explicit materials. Even then (1964) there was an abundance of evidence correlating the exhibition of obscene materials with sexually oriented crimes. During the next several years in whatever way possible I worked with Clancy in gathering evidence, signing complaints as a citizen litigant against the exhibition of obscene materials, and appearing before civic groups and governmental bodies to appeal for laws and government officials that would strengthen our efforts against these perversions. On many occasions people who should have been our strongest allies openly questioned our motives and our integrity.

It often proved to be a lonely, frustrating effort.

CHAPTER TWO

"I AM CURIOUS (YELLOW)"
"OH CALCUTTA"

In 1968 a blatantly pornographic film made in Sweden and entitled *I Am Curious (Yellow)* began to be exhibited in the United States. A number of states moved against the film and obtained judgments that it was pornographic. These courts ordered the forfeiture and confiscation of the film. In California the film began a series of exhibitions in the summer of 1969. In association with the film the producers distributed a 270-page book with photographic reproductions of scenes from the film and the associated dialogue. The film was clearly pornographic, depicting in graphic detail various scenes of human sexual activity and sexual perversion.

I wrote a series of letters to the appropriate law enforcement officials protesting their lack of action in prosecuting the exhibition of this blatantly obscene film. Finally, when it was obvious that none of the authorized and responsible officials would take action, Clancy and I filed a citizen's lawsuit against the film. Though I was at the time an elected public official, the lawsuit was filed in my capacity as a private citizen. In the lawsuit, *John Harmer v. A Motion Picture Entitled "I Am Curious (Yellow)* (Superior Court of the State of California for the County of Los Angeles, case number 967070), we cited the action of other states in declaring the film to be obscene. We also provided the court with excerpts from the film and from the published book showing scenes and dialogue from the film. Our petition asked that the court abate the film as a "public nuisance."

Within several days after the filing of our petition the law enforcement agencies suddenly awakened to the presence of the film and its outrageously pornographic nature. Throughout Los Angeles County various city and county entities proceeded to confiscate the film and to issue citations against its exhibitors. Had it not been for our efforts in the capacity of private citizens it is doubtful that formal action would have been taken by the responsible law enforcement agencies.

In an article published in the *Los Angeles Times* of December 31, 1969, the attorney who defended the various theaters exhibiting the film was quoted as saying that our action was part of " . . . a conspiracy against his clients sponsored by a group called Citizens Committee for Decent Literature" and that the action of the law enforcement agencies was "designed purely to harass my clients from conducting their business . . . the film is protected under the guarantees of the First Amendment." The fact that the film had been found in many jurisdictions outside of California to be patently obscene was deemed of little importance by this attorney. Indeed, as noted in the article, the film had also been "banned in Italy," of all places!

Our next effort against a pornographic production came when I received an urgent phone call from Jim Clancy. Could he come to see me about another pornographic presentation being exhibited in Los Angeles County? I agreed, and he immediately came to my office. Clancy got right to the point. A stage play had opened in Los Angeles called *Oh Calcutta*. It was, according to Clancy, "patently pornographic and violated several state and local statutes." Clancy wanted to shut it down, but needed to have a citizen plaintiff to assist him with the prosecution. Would I be willing to go to the production and carry with me a hidden camera that I would use to take photos of the nude actors on stage engaged in various acts of simulated sexual perversion?

Clancy was having serious problems with his superiors at the L.A. D.A.'s office. In recent weeks it had become clear that they were not nearly as supportive of his anti-pornography efforts as he needed them to be. Ordinarily a prosecutor would not need a "citizen plaintiff" to proceed on a matter that was as blatantly obscene as *Oh Calcutta*. However, as Clancy's efforts in Los Angeles County had begun to inflict more damage to the pornographers, they had managed to have their friends in the legitimate business community of L.A. put pressure on the D.A. to have Clancy assigned to some other tasks. At the time Clancy neglected to explain all of this to me, but later I learned just how powerful the pornography industry was with their ability to intimidate government officials.

Clancy did warn me that if I was caught taking the pictures I would likely be thrown out of the theater in a none too gentle manner. The original plan was that he would meet me outside after the show. For whatever reason, at the last minute he decided to buy a ticket and go in with me. To say that I was nervous and somewhat frightened would be an understatement in the extreme. Under those conditions, having the companionship of even a "bantam rooster" was somewhat comforting.

The so-called "play" was so pathetically devoid of any legitimate dramatic or humorous content that I found it difficult to understand why Clancy could not just shut it down for fraud on the basis of misrepresenting it to the buying public as a theatrical production. As it turned out, the audience couldn't have cared less about the paucity of any true artistic content. The so-called actors and actresses pranced their way through various scenes of nudity and simulated sexual acts. I was able to use Clancy's camera without being noted by the ushers, but there was no question that most of the people around me became conscious of what I was doing. I never did learn whether they were just amused, bemused, or jealous. At any rate, no one complained or turned me in to the management.

Those photos became pivotal as we initiated the effort to shut down the production. In order to explain what ultimately transpired I need to give some elementary background with regard to the legal framework within which a prosecutor had to work in order to effectively curtail or suppress a pornographic activity.

The statutory prohibitions against the exhibition of obscene productions were always subject to the case law decisions of the United States Supreme Court. That is, the statutes made the production and sale of pornography illegal, but the definition of what constituted an obscene or pornographic item came from the Court.

In 1964 the principal decision of the Supreme Court of the United States was known as "The Roth Case." This case was an

appeal from a conviction in the state of New York of one Samuel
Roth, who was an undisputed distributor of sexually morbid materials. As usual, the American Civil Liberties Union was in the forefront of Roth's defense, along with his own paid attorneys.

I shall not attempt to deal with all of the constitutional issues
involved in the Roth case, nor the various concurring and dissenting
opinions from the Court. The Court did affirm prior holdings that
obscenity as such did not have any right to protection under the First
Amendment to the Constitution. Having said that, however, the Court
then went on to try to define what constituted obscenity, and in this
effort the Roth decision literally gave an open door to the production
and distribution of obscene material in the United States.

In the *Roth* case the United States Supreme Court created a two-
headed monster with which prosecutors now had to deal in order to
obtain a conviction against a producer or distributor of pornography.
The effect of the Roth decision was to require that in the prosecution
of any obscene presentation or material the prosecutor must show
that "the dominant theme of the material, taken as a whole appeals to
a prurient interest in sex" and, "that the average person, applying
contemporary community standards, would find that the material was
patently offensive, and that the material, taken as a whole, appeals to
the prurient interest." For the next nine years the Roth decision would
be the dominant legal test for whether material could be considered
obscene.

In 1966 the Supreme Court expanded on a phrase first used in the
Roth case to add another nearly impossible requirement to the prosecutor's burden. In the case of *Memoirs v. Massachusetts,* the Court
restated the Roth criteria and made a specific requirement something
that had only been suggested in Roth. That was, now the prosecutor
had to show that the material " . . . is utterly without redeeming social
value." So now the prosecutor's burden was to convince the judge
and the jury that:

1. The dominant theme of the material taken as a whole appeals
   to a prurient interest in sex;
2. The material is patently offensive because it violates contemporary community standards relating to the description
   or representation of sexual matters; and

3. The material is "utterly" without redeeming social value.

In other words, to obtain a conviction against a pornographic item the prosecutor now had to show first that the item involved (book, magazine, motion picture) was "utterly without redeeming social importance"; second, that the material is obscene only if the dominant theme of the material, taken as a whole, appeals to the prurient interest; and third, that the first two requirements set forth above had to be determined on the basis that "to the average person, applying contemporary community standards, the dominant theme of the material taken as a whole appeals to the prurient interest."

The pornographers quickly saw in the Roth decision and later the Memoirs decision all that they needed to safely produce a plethora of new pornographic material. In order to avoid the "utterly without redeeming social value" test all the pornographers had to do was add portions of a play by Shakespeare or some other author, quote from some accepted authority on any social issue, or even, as some bla-tantly did, include chapters from the Bible in their materials. Some took a report to Congress on the issue of pornography and proceeded to illustrate it with vile photographs of the most lurid and degenerate scenes of sexual perversion. Since the publication included in total a report to the Congress of the United States from a presidentially appointed commission it could never be adjudged to be "utterly without redeeming social value."

The pornography industry now had an open door to a decade of fantastic profitability. In fact, the Roth and the Memoirs decisions created the phenomenon of the "Adult Theater" and the "Adult Book-store." For a period of time, until other means of profitably distrib-uting pornography became more widespread, the adult theaters and adult bookstores were the backbone of the pornographers' distribu-tion process.

The net effect of these criteria was to make it almost impossible for a prosecutor to successfully meet the Supreme Court's require-ments in order to obtain a conviction. Clancy's and my initial efforts against *Oh Calcutta* were soon doomed to failure because of the impossibility of meeting the Supreme Court's unattainable require-ments. So we began searching for an alternative legal theory that would effectively shut down the presentation.

The common law of England and the United States has for at least three centuries sustained the proposition that "Obscene or indecent exhibitions of a nature to shock the public sense of decency are also public nuisances and indictable at common law. This label includes not only obscene and indecent theatrical performances or 'side shows,' but other disgusting practices" (*Perkins, On Criminal Law;* 1st ed., 1957). Under that legal premise such "moral public nuisances" as houses of prostitution had been permanently enjoined and their revenues sequestered.

The legal theory that we used against *I Am Curious (Yellow)* and *Oh Calcutta* came from the California Penal Code provisions regarding "A Public Nuisance." We initially lost both cases before the Supreme Court of the state of California. The court at that time was dominated by liberal jurists who had no sympathy for our efforts. In a 4-3 decision written by ultra-liberal Justice Stanley Mosk, the court defeated both of our efforts. The court's action was approvingly summarized in an article of February 2, 1970, appearing in the entertainment industry publication *Variety,* which noted as follows:

> Majority decisions in Friday's ruling said live plays in a theatre are protected under the First Amendment just as are motion pictures, magazines and newspapers. It went on to say (sic) basic purpose of the penal code section under question is to punish the crime of vagrancy-not theatrical performances.* Majority opinion was written by Stanley Mosk.
>
> Dissenting opinion, penned by Justice Louis Burke, said the decision's effect is "to allow acts, however obscene, to be performed on the stage with complete freedom unless they are proscribed by other laws.
>
> Whether the specific ruling will extend to films is not clear, but should soon be learned, as "Oh Calcutta" is involved in a suit along with the Swedish film, "I Am Curious (Yellow)" by State Senator John L. Harmer (R-Glendale). Harmer has a people's suit against the two properties pending in Superior Court, charging both with being public nuisances, obscene and in violation of the state's law against obscenity. It would clearly seem that the latter two charges were nullified by the Supreme Court ruling.

*<u>Note</u>: This comment referred to our having brought our

action in civil law, not criminal law, on the theory that the presentation of the stage play was a "moral public nuisance" and as a citizen who was damaged by the presence of the nuisance I petitioned the court to have it abated (removed or destroyed).

Pornography primarily exists for one reason: it is highly profitable. While the pornographers can rely upon the human tendency to be attracted to the morbid, the bizarre, the carnal, the sexually explicit, the fact is that without the ability to prey on these mortal characteristics in a financially lucrative manner there would be little effort made to produce and distribute pornography. It has always been possible to make a significant amount of money from pornography, even when most of it was technically shoddy and so primitive in its production as to be twenty years behind the times in the quality of its printed or filmed presentation. With the vast expansion of the market for pornographic material the producers have been able to utilize the most modern printing and motion picture technology to bring to the market a product using the finest procedures. Back in 1964 this was still not the situation, even though the profit incentive was all-compelling.

Clancy figured that if we could find a legal theory that would take the profitability out of the presentation of *Oh Calcutta,* we could win the day. Instead of fighting with the Supreme Court's ponderous and impossible task of meeting the Roth and Memoirs criteria, we sought for a legal process to take the profit out·of the production. We found our answer in the common law doctrine applicable to a "public nuisance." Under centuries of British and American common law the courts had held that one may not be allowed to profit from maintaining a public nuisance. If it was determined that a certain activity constituted a public nuisance, the plaintiff, or the people through their attorney general, could sequester all of the revenue associated with the public nuisance as a means of curtailing its continued presence.

In the midst of this effort Clancy was given an ultimatum by his superiors at the Los Angeles D.A. office. He had to "back off" much of his current investigation of the production and distribution of pornography, or be reassigned to other duties. As he always did, Clancy simply took the course of action consistent with his own sense of integrity and honor. He resigned.

Now we were without the ability to proceed on behalf of the people through their criminal prosecutor. Whatever was to be done would have to be accomplished in a civil complaint brought by myself as a citizen with Clancy as my attorney.

In *Harmer v. Oh Calcutta*, Clancy was able to identify the legal theory that we needed, that is, the private citizen's standing to file suit in order to abate the continued presence of a "moral public nuisance." However, it took us several more efforts in various courts around California before we successfully persuaded the court that the presentation—whether technically obscene or not under the Supreme Court's definition—was a presentation that constituted a "moral" public nuisance. As such, the plaintiff had a right to sequester the income that came through the continued maintenance of the public nuisance.

Oh Calcutta was taken to the city of Fresno. There we obtained the assistance of several residents who had worked with me in other similar efforts, notably Blaine Thomas, Curtis Cole, and Lloyd Harline. By the time we filed the suit in Fresno we had modified the complaint to meet the objections to our legal theory previously raised by the courts. This time the court ruled in our favor and ordered the play closed and the proceeds sequestered on the basis that the play constituted a "moral public nuisance."

The day the court handed down that opinion was the last time that *Oh Calcutta* was presented in California.

Chapter Three

HOW THE MOTION PICTURE
RATING SYSTEM CAME TO BE

In 1966 I was elected to the California state senate as the senator from the twenty-first district, located entirely within Los Angeles County. The district, composed of over seven hundred thousand people, was predominantly conservative in its political orientation. That fact made it possible for me to pursue a legislative agenda that was based on the values and principles that had always been a part of my life as a Latter-day Saint.

The year 1966 was also the year that Ronald Reagan was first elected governor of California. I had known Reagan for nearly four years, having first met him in 1962 when I arranged for him to be the featured speaker at a campaign event for a congressional candidate for whom I was campaign manager. After that initial meeting we had both corresponded and spoken directly about his ultimate entry onto the political scene as a candidate. From those communications it had become apparent to me that Reagan, even in 1962, knew exactly where he wanted to go in the political process. He would run for governor in 1966 as a conservative Republican. (In 1962 he was still a registered Democrat.)

For the two years prior to my election I had spent nearly half of my time working with Clancy on various anti-pornography efforts. We had no money, and no deep-pocket sponsor behind us, so we were often prevented by lack of financial resources from doing things that needed to be done. Still, we managed to engage in enough of the battle that we got to know the enemy, and as was first pronounced in the famous comic strip by Walt Kelly, Pogo, "We have met the enemy—and they are us." As a member of the California state senate I soon came to realize how truly insightful Walt Kelley's little character, Pogo, really was. On many occasions I would meet "the enemy" sitting right at my elbow.

Pornographic material is essentially perverted fantasy. The pornographer presents sexual material in the grossest and crassest expression of physical and sexual experience. Then as the appetite of the viewer increases for more degenerate depictions of sexual conduct, and the individual's sensitivity decreases, various forms of deviant sexual perversions are introduced. Finally, increasing forms of violence associated with sexual conduct that are referred to as "sado-masochistic" material is offered by the pornographer. The ultimate obscenity comes with a sexually oriented torture session that ends in the literal filmed death and even dismemberment of the victim.

It is important to understand the distinction between what is referred to as "hard core" pornography and "soft-core" pornography. This same distinction also has much to do with whether a motion picture is X-rated or R-rated.

A motion picture is only considered "hard core" or X-rated if either the male or female genitalia is shown in a sexually explicit close-up or there is a close-up of penetration in the sex scenes. Otherwise, lacking such close-up specificity, it is considered "soft core" and may even be allowed to have the R rating, notwithstanding the fact that the film exhibits very explicit sexual intercourse scenes that are presented with full nudity. Absent a close-up view of penetration, the intercourse scenes are considered "simulated" rather than actual.

Thus when the motion picture *Young Lady Chatterly* was shown over Utah cable television a series of intercourse scenes was presented in total nudity. Even though the nude couple are in a full intercourse embrace it is referred to as "simulated" rather than actual intercourse because there is no close-up of the penetration. Thus it is R rated.

The people who produced pornography ranged across the spectrum from the powerful Mafia families in organized crime to slovenly one-man operations working in a garage somewhere in Los Angeles.

But they were only part of the enemy. I soon came to understand that no one did more to further the work of the pornography industry in America than the motion picture industry, the slick magazine publishers, and their ever-present lackeys, the ACLU.

The motion picture industry, through their minions in Hollywood, always made certain that the ACLU was very generously funded. Hollywood luminaries fell all over themselves to host fundraising events for the ACLU, often obtaining large crowds of attendees at a cost of as much as five thousand dollars per person. Between Hollywood and New York City the funding made available to the ACLU was in the millions of dollars. The ACLU in turn was ever present at the court house, in the legislative chambers, and throughout the media, with well-paid teams of lawyers to fight against any effort to control the increasingly degenerate materials finding their way onto the silver screen.

The real benefit of the ACLU to the pornography industry, however, was not the quality of their legal talent. The greatest benefit to the pornographers from the participation of the ACLU was the totally false assertion that this was an "independent party" with no financial interest in the outcome of the lawsuit, but whose only interest was to "defend the rights guaranteed by the First Amendment." Nothing could have been farther from the truth. The ACLU was bought and paid for by those very interests they were so willing to defend.

The motion picture industry was engaged every bit as much in a secret conspiracy of deceit and destruction as later evidence proved the tobacco industry to be so engaged. They were ever aided and abetted, both financially and in powerful reams of propaganda, by the slick magazine publishers. We also had to contend with the malicious characterization of our efforts by the reporters in the daily press. In every one of the anti-pornography efforts in which I was ever involved this combination of financial and political power along with the propaganda power of the media were ever-present to oppose our efforts. It is little wonder that we almost never won. The odds against us were overwhelming.

During my years in public office I continued in my anti-pornography efforts, along with a deep involvement with the public schools and the issues of economic development for California. My constituents always supported my efforts, and my percentage margin of victory at the polls grew larger with each re-election to the state senate. After three or four years of frustrating defeats in the courts, I resolved to proceed with a legislative package that would give local prosecutors the statutes they needed to effectively fight against pornography. I felt that we could proceed with a legislative package that would completely meet the state and federal constitutional requirements and be effective in protecting our society from the smut peddlers.

In 1970 the Republican members of the state senate elected me their caucus chairman. In that capacity I received increased loyalty from many of my associates in the senate and worked almost daily with Governor Reagan and his staff on their legislative priorities. I became the designated spokesman for the governor's legislative program in the senate, and continued in that role until my appointment by Governor Reagan as lieutenant governor in 1974.

Notwithstanding my increased influence in the senate, the pornographers and their friends were ever able to intercept and destroy most of my efforts in the other house of the legislature, the state assembly. In 1968 I introduced Senate Bill 372 in the California senate, a bill that would create "The California Motion Picture Review Board." This state entity would be charged with the responsibility of rating motion pictures on their suitability for family viewing. The commission would develop a rating system that would have to be used with the advertising and promotion of any motion picture being exhibited in the state. The objective was to create a state agency that would be a totally independent and reliable source of information for parents as to the suitability of any given motion picture for viewing by their children.

The Motion Picture Association of America (MPAA) moved quickly to defeat the measure. However, I had been able to mobilize sufficient support in the senate to assure its passage out of that house. It was at that moment that the industry came forward with an irresistible proposal. The office of the legislative analyst had inserted in the bill an estimated annual cost to the state of $500,000. Given the scope of the commission's task, that was not an unreasonable estimate. Given the potential benefit to the people of the state, that was a very inexpensive way to help protect the moral values of our youth.

The Motion Picture Association came forward and said, in effect, that if the senate would hold my bill in committee the industry promised to develop the very proposal contained in the bill but at the sole expense of the industry. There would be no cost to the taxpayers of the state.

It did not require any great depth of intellect to see the obvious— the fox was offering to guard the henhouse at no expense to the owner of the chickens. I warned my colleagues of what would obviously take place The industry would simply use and distort the rating system to their own benefit. Instead of protecting families from the destructive and insidious erosion of moral values that the industry was intentionally pursuing, the rating system would become a false source of evaluation telling parents that a film was suitable for viewing by their children when in fact it was filled with the very degenerate materials that they feared. The industry would use their rating system to legitimatize degeneracy instead of suppress it.

The senate gullibly swallowed the motion picture industry's story. My bill was held in committee and, as the industry promised, they came forward with their own rating system. My predictions, on this and a number of other matters, were soon verified. Today the so-called motion picture rating system is not only a travesty; it is affirmatively used to enhance the market acceptance of a motion picture.

Today, films that would otherwise have been left free of perversion are now intentionally filled with nudity and violence in order to obtain the so-called R rating. The so-called R rating was represented by the MPAA as a means of preventing anyone under the age of eighteen from viewing motion pictures that were only "suitable" for adult audiences. This assertion was typical of the hypocrisy of the MPAA. To begin with, there never was any effort to exclude someone under the age of eighteen from the theater. More significantly, however, was the way the MPAA consistently used the R rating to increase the degree of violence and explicit sexuality depicted in the motion pictures.

So successful was the MPAA's strategy that soon it became necessary to increase the degree of graphic violence and sexual titillation in order to assure an audience for the film. Now the R rating guarantees an audience who otherwise would likely ignore a film that could not promise their being satiated with graphic portrayals of sexual violence and profanity.

There is absolutely no effort to enforce the supposed exclusion from the theater of youth below the age of eighteen for R rated films, or below the age of 13 for the PG-13 rating. The motion picture industry's rating system promised to protect families from vile and degenerate materials. It has done exactly the opposite.

It took even less time than I had predicted for the pornographers to be able to effectively utilize the motion picture industry's "self-policing program" for their own purposes. The following quote is from the slick tabloid publication of the motion picture industry, *Variety,* dated August 9, 1972: "American Int'l Pictures and Sherpix Inc. each have scrubbed up two former X-rated jobs, which have come somewhat bleached from the laundromat with R rating. The Sherpix film is the 3-D 'The Stewardesses,' which made millions as an X pic. And is now making the rounds as an R. AIP's 'The Dirtiest Girl I Ever Met' (see 'Oh Carol') now wears an R label."

In an article by *Deseret News* film critic Christopher Hicks in the Sunday, October 16, 1983 *Deseret News* entitled "Has 'Thou Shalt Not' Become Thou Shalt?" Mr. Hicks offers the following comment from a fellow film critic, Mr. Vernon Scott, of UPI: "UPI's Hollywood reporter Vernon Scott, for example, calls the R rating 'a national joke,' because of its lack of enforcement. And since so many PG and R films seem interchangeable, in terms of content, and because the G and X are virtually extinct among main-stream movies today, other critics suggest the entire system be scrapped.

"When a movie like 'The Verdict,' carries the same R rating as 'Porkys' or 'Escape 2000,' and when vulgar movies like 'Smokey and the Bandit, Part 3' and sexy/violent movies like 'Never Say Never Again' have the same PG rating as 'Mr Mom,' it does cause a certain amount of wonderment."

In reality there is no need for "wonderment" at all. The Motion Picture Association of America blatantly uses the rating system to market movies, not to enable parents to know what may be harmful to their children or offensive to their own moral values.

On a much broader basis the motion picture industry used the R rating as justification for including in films nudity, simulated sex, violence, and profanity. What the industry's rating system had done was legitimatize these features in a film because the rating system allowed a film with that content to be distributed as long as the R rating was prominently shown. Now films that would have otherwise found no need for obscenity continually seek out the inclusion of sex and violence in the film to assure the maximum audience. The motion picture industry's perversion of the rating system has been exactly what the pornographers wanted.

Noted Latter-day Saint motion picture producer and director Kieth Merrill wrote an editorial piece published in the *Deseret News* on Saturday, March 21, 1998, on the subject of the abuse of the ratings system by the MPAA.

> There seems to be a widespread perception among Latter-day Saints that the Church's policy on films begins and ends with: "Don't go to R-rated movies." Despite admonitions from the general pulpit to use discernment in the selection of all films, videos and television programming, this singular advice has taken deep root.
>
> The result is an attachment to the shifting secular standard of the Motion Picture Association of America's rating system that was unintended.
>
> In 1986, then-church President Ezra Taft Benson said: "We counsel you young men . . . don't see R-rated movies or vulgar videos or participate in any entertainment that is immoral, suggestive or pornographic."
>
> Other LDS general authorities gave similar counsel following the establishment of the MPAA's rating system in November 1968. Still, President Benson's pointed exhortation, "don't see R-rated movies" had the effect of elevating the admonition to the status of official church policy, if not doctrine.
>
> By implication, parents, teachers and Church members inadvertently adopted the rating system of the MPAA as consistent with the standard of the Church, or at least a reliable guideline for their entertainment choices.
>
> Fingering R-rated films as culprits unintentionally granted PG and PG-13 films a kind of tacit approval, especially among teenagers. But that is not what was said. It is not what was intended. It is simply what happened, and it is a connection I believe should be broken.
>
> The PG-13 rating had been around less than two years when

President Benson issued his trenchant advice. The "vulgar videos" he denounced are often rated PG-13.

A recent case in point: "In & Out" is a popular and enormously successful PG-13 film. It has gained renewed fame with an Academy Award-nominated performance. *Entertainment Magazine*'s cover feature called it: "In & Out-rageous How the Surprise Smash—and its shocking kiss—is turning Gay into Gold." . . .

But dissected, the film is little more than 104 minutes of propaganda for the homosexual lifestyle.

The title itself, derived from a disturbing dialogue among teenage boys who explain homosexual acts using conspicuous euphemisms, is shocking when reexamined in the cold light of day.

As Kieth Merrill's article effectively notes, the MPAA has simply used the motion picture rating system as a means of legitimatizing in the minds of many the propagandizing of immorality and obscenity. There is no way that responsible parents could or should use the motion picture rating system as the determinative factor in whether a motion picture is suitable for their family.

In the next year (1969) I pursued two other legislative efforts related to pornography, both of which were intensely opposed by the same adversaries: the ACLU, the motion picture industry, and the slick magazine publishers and distributors. One had to do with the hideous increase in pornography that exploited children (Senate Bill 83 of the 1969 session.) The other (Senate Bill 1419) took the Supreme Court decisions in Roth and Memoirs and reduced them to a statutory enactment that would at least give prosecutors some basis for confidence in pursuing the constantly expanding presence of adult theaters, bookstores, and so on.

Senate Bill 83 made it a crime to sell any book or magazine containing drawings or photographs or to produce or distribute a film or filmstrip which "portrays a nude child or adolescent of either sex in a pose or position designed or intended to appeal to the sexual curiosity or the prurient interest of the purchaser."

After my first contact in 1964 with the pornographic material being published, the law enforcement officers who frequently came to my office brought reports of a dramatic increase in the amount of "pedophelia," or obscene material involving the exploitation of children or youth. State and federal law enforcement personnel and prosecutors involved with pornography were finding a dramatic increase in the amount of this material. Corresponding to that increase in the material being produced was the rapidly increasing incidence of child molestation, child abuse, and child exploitation for sexual purposes. The pedophelia materials were being sold at unbelievable prices to a rapidly expanding group of perverted individuals (not always exclusively men) whose morhidity had centered on the depiction of children or youth in deviant sexuality.

Predictably both bills (Senate Bill 83 and Senate Bill 1419) were defeated. Obviously no one would come forward to oppose the bills on the basis that they were in favor of pornography. Invariably the first words spoken by their hapless witnesses would be to the effect, "We (the ACLU, the motion picture industry, the magazine publishers and distributors) are opposed to pornography. . . . But these bills have a serious danger of attacking constitutionally protected rights of free speech, etc., etc., etc." Their perfidy and duplicity were always presented with a straight face, even though everyone present in the hearing room, everyone, knew how outrageously untrue such representations were. Particularly gullible were the librarians, whom the ACLU marched in like so many sheep to recite their propaganda.

These witnesses gave the legislators who were afraid to offend these powerful interests the excuse they needed to vote against the proposed legislation. The lies and misrepresentations were always the same. No matter how many highly qualified witnesses with outstanding credentials in the areas of constitutional law and behavioral science were present to testify in support of the measures, the pornographers would win the day. As legitimate scholars such as Dr. Victor Cline, and others, came to testify in support of the bills, they could hardly believe their ears at the distortion of truth regarding the negative effects of pornography, the law, and the Constitution that came from the testimony of the witnesses who fronted for the pornographers.

In the end it was the financial power of the motion picture industry that made the difference. I spent more than three years of my seven years in the California state senate as the Chairman of the

Republican caucus. I was the governor's spokesman on the senate floor and the individual responsible for raising campaign contributions for the members of the caucus. I knew who was taking money from the MPAA representatives and what commitments they made to get it.

The motion picture producers and their spokesmen wanted nothing on the books that could keep them from moving farther and farther into the pornographers' domain. As their conspiracy to erode and destroy the public's commitment to decency went forward it was imperative for their financial success that there be nothing in the law that could impair their ability to exploit indecency and obscenity. They knew exactly where they wanted to go, and that was to occupy the spectrum of sexuality that the pornographers had abandoned in order to go further to the extreme.

The motion picture industry wanted and needed the pornographers to continue unabated so that the pornographers could continue to push the "community standards of decency" farther into the mire. In turn, the pornographers needed the motion picture industry to create an ever-expanding market for their wares by developing an appetite for sexually explicit materials in people who previously had never been induced to seek the same. The symbiotic relationship between the two was ever more evident at every confrontation regarding an attempt to protect the dignity and standard of decency in the community.

In the fall of 1978 I was one of the faculty lecturing at a conference of prosecutors who were still committed to contending with the pornographers. One of the other individuals there to make a presentation was a recently retired agent of the Federal Bureau of Investigation. He shared with me the details behind a recent meeting of the pornography industry's principal members. At that meeting a presentation was made by a highly regarded, nationally known management consulting firm who had been retained by this group to outline for them a marketing and distribution strategy for the next ten years. The report that was presented was based on extensive research and market analysis. In summary, the report stated that "to significantly increase revenue for the pornographers the following things would have to be done:

1. Dramatically improve the aesthetic quality of the product.
2. Make the product accessible in the home without the need for patronizing the "adult theater" or the "adult bookstore" in public view.
3. Develop a marketing strategy that would make pornography acceptable to women.
4. Use the motion picture industry to create an attitude of casual acceptance of explicit sexual material.
5. And finally, most perceptively, introduce a camouflage into the presentation of the pornography in the form of humor and/or presentations of dramatic human endeavor.

In other words, if you could associate pornography with laughter or drama the explicit sexuality would be overlooked as a necessary component of the presentation.

In the twenty years since that conversation I have watched the strategy unfold with incredible speed. Taking advantage of new technology and the willing cooperation of the motion picture industry, the pornographers now have access to every living room in America.

CHAPTER FOUR

CENSORSHIP
AND A FREE SOCIETY

————————

With our success against *Oh Calcutta,* Clancy felt he had found a legal theory that the courts would accept without having to deal with the impossible burden of the Supreme Court's criteria for proving an item to be obscene. On many occasions I continued as much as possible to work with Clancy, and to act as the plaintiff when needed, or the attorney of record when that was useful.

In 1970 I was blessed with the addition to my staff of one of the purest and most honorable men I have ever met—Ernie Schulzke. Ernie was married to my cousin Margo Seymour. A graduate of the University of Chicago school of law, he was a brilliant legal scholar as well as a wonderfully meek human being. Ernie had left the practice of law and had been teaching as an institute and seminary instructor in the Church Educational System. I had known and admired him for many years, not only for his keen intellect but also for his deep sense of integrity and his unswerving loyalty to truth and virtue.

Thus it was that in 1969 I approached Ernie about leaving the CES and coming to join my staff. To my great delight and benefit he agreed to the proposal. I now felt that I had at my right hand someone who could deal with the most critical legal and philosophical issues involved in all aspects of my legislative agenda. I never had cause to regret my decision.

With Ernie Schulzke providing the staff support for the legislative efforts, and Jim Clancy as the attorney in the courtroom efforts, the years 1967 through 1973 were an intense period of seeking to throw back the tidal wave of vile and obscene material that was being produced in California and distributed throughout the country. In chapter 6 I outline more completely the legislative effort that culminated in 1972 with a series of bills in the California Senate and a statewide ballot proposition. In the courtroom our efforts met with enough success to keep us going but never enough to provide a decisive victory. And ever and always there was the miserable problem of how to finance our efforts.

With the successful closing of the obscene stage performance called *Oh Calcutta*, achieved on the basis of the common law doctrine of abating a public nuisance, we decided to use that legal mechanism to attack some of the pornographic motion pictures that had come into circulation.

We initiated a series of lawsuits with myself as the plaintiff and Jim Clancy as the attorney. Among these were *Harmer v. Tonylyn Productions* (23 Cal App. 3d 941) against the exhibition of a film entitled *Without A Stitch; Harmer* v. *Deep Throat* (Los Angeles Superior Court No. C 63814, Sept. 1973); *Harmer* v. *The Devil in Miss Jones* (California Court of Appeals, Second Appellate District, No. 43778, 1976); and *Harmer vs. Busch* (17 Cal. 3d at 49). We also supplied other prosecutors and citizen groups around the country with briefs and memoranda that enabled them to pursue similar litigation against these and other films.

Though our common law abatement strategy was used successfully against these and other films in several states, in California the court continually held against us. The dissenting opinion of Justice Herndon in the Court of Appeals, Second District, Division 2, of March 2, 1972, outlined effectively the basis of our approach. Justice Herndon, in a strongly worded dissent in which he sought to sustain our complaint seeking to enjoin the exhibition of the film, *Without A Stitch,* summarized the content of the film very succinctly: "The English language does not provide adjectives sufficient to describe the utter rottenness of this sordid product of sub-human depravity and greed that portrays every known form of sexual perversion."

We had supplied the court with photographic evidence of the content of the film(s). Justice Herndon noted that "The film *Without*

A Stitch is hard-core pornography as defined in Section 311, Subdivision (a), of the Penal Code and is beyond Constitutional protection." He then went on to note that the exhibition of such a hard-core pornographic motion picture created a public nuisance. He noted that our brief and allegations were "sufficient to satisfy pleading requirements with respect to the element of special injury which is essential to establish appellants' capacity to maintain the action under Civil Code section 3493."

With the facts and the law so overwhelmingly on our side we kept asking the question, "How can we lose?" Yet lose we did, though never on the basis of the actual issue of whether or not the films were hard-core pornography. No one, not even the most liberal fuzzy-minded jurist on the bench, could have doubted that these films constituted hard-core pornography. The majority always found something with which to deny us the petition to abate the exhibition as a public nuisance and to sequester the revenue obtained therefrom. In this instance, the majority decided that showing the film in a closed theater to "willing paying customers" negated the public nuisance argument. However, as we and Judge Herndon noted, the same legal theory had been sustained in closing red light district houses of prostitution, even though they were equally enclosed and frequented by "willing paying customers."

For several years we continued our efforts to develop a strategy under the common law of nuisance doctrine that would allow the citizen the right to go into court and remove the obscene items from his community. We filed two separate civil lawsuits in the Los Angeles County Superior Court in an effort to have the two pornographic films *Deep Throat* and *Devil in Miss Jones* declared to be hard-core pornography and moral public nuisances and their exhibition in the community to be unlawful under California law.

After three years of litigation, including two successive appeals to the California Supreme Court and one petition to the United States Supreme Court for a hearing in each of the two cases, two separate divisions of the California Court of Appeals handed down two conflicting decisions. In the *Deep Throat* case, one court of appeal held that only a city attorney or a district attorney could bring such an action, and that a private citizen such as myself did not have standing to litigate that issue in the courtroom. In the *Devil in Miss Jones* appeal a second division of the same court of appeal held that it might be possible for a private citizen to allege sufficient facts to establish private injury to property and thus state a cause of action, but ruled that the plaintiff would have to start all over in the trial court and amend the pleading to see if he could correct the defect as to standing.

In each of these cases the courts had before them photographic time-and-motion studies that showed the immutable hard-core nature of the films themselves. The California Supreme Court refused to rule on which of the two decisions was the correct law in the state of California.

One of the important aspects of the strategy of using the public nuisance statutes in fighting pornography was the fact that they gave the citizen the ability to fight against pornography when the responsible law enforcement officials declined to do so. In all fairness it must be noted that the reticence of the law enforcement people was not because they were sympathetic with pornography. Their ignoring of the pornographic films was simply an admission of the miserably complicated procedures that had to be followed to prosecute pornography. With their resources strained to maintain "law and order" as it was, taking on the exhibition of a motion picture (even one that was patently obscene and so held by responsible state and federal courts in other parts of the country) was simply not a priority. When a lone citizen began to utilize the available processes of the courts to fight a battle that the responsible law enforcement officials were hoping to ignore, they could no longer pretend that it was not there.

During the course of our efforts we did obtain one encouraging victory in the California State Supreme Court. We had persuaded the district attorney of Los Angeles County to allow us to file on his behalf a petition in the Superior Court that would recognize the authority of the district attorney to proceed in a non-criminal civil proceeding to close an adult theater as a "moral public nuisance." The court ruled in the case, known as *People ex rel. Busch v. Projection Room Theater, et al,* (17 Cal. 3d 42, 130 Cal. Reporter 328), that a theater which regularly showed pornographic films and a book store that regularly sold pornographic materials "was a public nuisance which could be abated in a civil lawsuit filed by a City Attorney or a District Attorney." It was a small first step in a process that we had been pursuing for more than six years, and which we continued to pursue elsewhere in the country with increasing success. Then the Internet appeared and made the adult theater and bookstore relatively obsolete.

It is not the object of this book to provide a legal treatise on the law of obscenity. Rather, my purpose is to give an outline of the sequence of events that have transpired over the last thirty years and have now brought us to a time that can only be described as one in which a vast number of the people are "ripened in iniquity" (Ether 2:9-10; 9:20). Later in this book I shall outline what has now become available to anyone on the Internet and note the documented evidence of the extensive number of patrons of the Internet Web sites for pornography. It is not for me to predict when the Lord will determine that His criteria of being ripened in iniquity as set forth in the scriptures has been met. There are places in America today, however, that have already surpassed Sodom and Gomorrah for evil.

Ever present in all of our courtroom battles was the ACLU, acting as "amicus" or "friend of the court" petitioners on behalf of the pornographers. Whether the judges and juries were always totally deceived by this pretended separation of interests was never certain, but more often than not the deception worked. Never mind the fact that the overwhelming majority of the ACLU financing came from the very people who were producing and distributing the pornography. The arguments in support of the pornographers were always couched in language involving the First Amendment rights of freedom of speech. As many a courageous dissenting judge noted, no one could remotely conceive of a loss of free speech through the restriction of the production and distribution of this vile material. Still, the downhill slide seemed destined to accelerate and continue unabated.

What are these "ideas" that it is so critical for the ACLU to protect? We are not referring to simple erotic fantasy where heterosexual activity is taking place. The presentations that the ACLU was required to protect for their financial supporters included the most deviant and perverted of sexual conduct, often associated with sadomasochistic violence. There are no "ideas" here that are in danger of suppression. There is only the degenerate, vulgar, crude exploitation of sexual deviancy.

Some additional minor victories did come our way. The United States Supreme Court finally revisited the issue of what criteria was necessary to establish that a matter was obscene and subject to abatement or total suppression by the state. In June of 1973, some sixteen years after the Roth decision, the Supreme Court handed down decisions involving a group of obscenity laws that slightly eased the burden on the prosecution with regard to proving a matter to be obscene. The principal case in the group was *Miller v. California.*

Miller was an active distributor of pornographic materials and in this instance was charged with soliciting the purchase of pornography through materials sent through the United States Postal Service. The brochures advertising his pornographic products contained sexually explicit material and were mailed randomly to what the court referred to as "unwilling recipients." The Supreme Court decided to use the Miller case to restate the definition of pornography. It was a well-intentioned effort, but the results were a mixed bag for the prosecutors.

The Court retained the essential elements of the Roth and Memoirs decisions with one notable exception. Instead of requiring that the allegedly obscene material must be "utterly without redeeming social value," the Court specifically rejected that criterion and substituted for it the finding that the material was obscene if "the work, taken as a whole, lacks serious literary, artistic, political, or scientific value."

The other change made by the Court in the Miller case was the requirement that the statute by which the defendant was prosecuted must clearly state the type of obscene depiction that was considered to be obscene and subject to prosecution. This requirement by the court was precisely what I had attempted with a package of legislation pursued during the 1972 legislative year and with Proposition 18 on the California statewide ballot in November of 1972. Both the legislation and the proposition were attacked by the usual wolf pack composed of the ACLU, the motion picture industry, and the magazine publishers and distributors on the basis of the fact that they went contrary to the Supreme Court's prior holdings. In fact, the Miller case confirmed that the Court expected the very thing we were attempting to accomplish.

With the removal of the "utterly without redeeming social value" test, for the first time in nearly two decades prosecutors were able to start winning small victories in the prosecution of adult theaters, porno parlors and bookstores, and thinly disguised houses of prostitution called massage parlors. But even as these small victories began to give us hope that we could remove the blight of obscene and pornographic material from the American scene, technological developments were taking place that would ultimately change the entire marketing approach of the pornographers. As noted earlier, the pornographers had set as a goal the ability to "market" directly into the home, so that the public eye of disapproval that deterred the customer of the "adult theater" and bookstore could be overcome. In addition the pornographers wanted to find a way to make their product acceptable to women and to begin the process of addiction to pornography at a much younger age. As they worked to achieve these three goals there came into the market place the video cassette player and recorder.

Nothing could have been more advantageous to the pornographers. Now obscenity could be seen and exhibited entirely in the privacy of the home. All of the salacious and sleazy materials that had successfully been attacked in the courts and found to be in violation of common law and statutory prohibitions could now be purchased and carried home in small brown bags. The potential profits, which had always been so irresistible to the pornographers, now substantially increased as every home in America became a potential porno theater.

At the same time the motion picture industry continued to move farther and farther into the realm of explicit sexual content. The effect was to both desensitize the public to the lewdness and indecency of what was being offered and at the same time to create an appetite for more and more motion pictures depicting explicit sexual conduct. Thus, just when the courts had at last begun to acknowledge the validity of our legal theories and the reality of the danger posed to our society as testified to by various authentic expert witnesses, the entire arena changed. The adult theaters became obsolete and soon diminished in number. The adult bookstore still thrives, but the monopoly on the market that it once held for printed material has disappeared. Today pornographic materials can be obtained through other sources without the public scrutiny that comes from one's going to an identified source such as the adult bookstore. The sale of the pornographic videocassette in addition to the printed material sustains most of the adult bookstores.

It is important to understand that not all opposition to the suppression of pornography comes from mean-spirited hypocrites such as the attorneys who defend the pornographers. There are very serious and credible arguments to support the requirement to constantly be on guard against the loss of essential liberties, of which freedom of speech is the foundation. What the zealots of anti-censorship seem to never grasp is how quickly and effectively pornography "sleazes" over the line into that which has no legitimate right for protection under the guise of freedom of speech.

Robert Bork is widely acknowledged, even by those who disagree with him, as one of the most brilliant legal minds and jurists of this century. One of the many political tragedies of our times was the successful opposition to his nomination to the Supreme Court of the United States by a combination of all the liberal entities in the country. With regard to the issue of "censorship" and the First Amendment, Bork, ever the scholar but also the keen observer of democratic institutions, wrote as follows:

> It will be said that to propose banning anything that can be called "expression" is an attempt to "take away our constitutional rights." . . . Until quite recently, nobody even raised the question of that [the First] amendment in prosecutions of pornographers; it was not thought relevant even by the pornographers. As late as 1942, in the *Chaplinsky* decision, a unanimous Supreme Court could agree:
> "There are certain well-defined and narrowly limited classes of speech, the prevention and punishment of which have never been thought to raise any Constitutional problems. These include the lewd and obscene, the profane, the libelous, and the insulting or 'fighting' words—those which by their very utterance inflict injury or tend to incite an immediate breach of the peace. It has been well observed that

such utterances are no essential part of any exposition of ideas, and are
of such slight social value as a step to truth that any benefit that may be
derived from them is clearly outweighed by the social interest in order
and morality."

  ' Under today's constitutional doctrine, it would be difficult to
impossible to prohibit or punish the lewd and obscene, or the profane.
First Amendment jurisprudence has shifted from the protection of the
exposition of ideas towards the protection of self-expression—however
lewd, obscene, or profane. . . .

  Yet it is clear that if there is something special about speech, something that warrants a constitutional guarantee, *it is the capacity of
speech to communicate ideas.* . . . The only difference between speech
and other behavior is speech's capacity to communicate ideas in the
effort to reach varieties of truth. Celebration in song of the ripping of
vaginas or forced oral sex or stories depicting the kidnapping, mutila-
tion, raping, and murder of children do not, to anyone with a degree of
common sense, qualify as ideas. (Robert Bork, *Slouching Towards
Gomorrah* [New York: Regan Books, 1996], pp. 147–48; emphasis
added.)

The fundamental distinction that these people never seem to
admit is that obscenity and pornography never present an "idea" as
such, except as a camouflage for the presentation of the erotic material. Sometimes the defenders of pornography will attempt to conceal
their vile presentations under the guise of the expression of "love."
Invariably and without exception the real intent of the presentation
and the effect of their material is to arouse lust and passion that has
nothing to do with the human emotion of love. Pornography never
can and never will be equivalent to the expression of genuine affection, tenderness, and human emotional attachment. Anyone who has
viewed pornography even in its most elementary forms soon comes
to realize that it is the exact opposite of those expressions of human
emotion that are consistent with tenderness and love.

Consider the most frequent form of elementary pornography, the
graphic depiction of the human genitals. There is nothing in such
depictions that conveys any of the human emotions that are defensible as essential to the bonding of a man and woman in the marital
union. The women and men who are depicted in such exhibitions are

in fact denigrated into subhuman objects for exploitation. When one gets to the more vicious forms of pornography there is the added factor of extreme violence and the brutalization of bizarre sexual conduct. Yet these examples of the pornographer's wares invariably and without exception quickly follow on the footsteps of the more elementary forms of obscenity, the graphic presentation of the private parts of the human body even without overt sexual conduct.

The dilemma for the parent, the religious leader, and the political activist is how to make the case for the danger of that which, though textually arousing and titillating, is too much an accepted part of our "arts" and "entertainment" to be susceptible to legal action as obscene. Thanks to the intentional efforts of the motion picture industry, we now accept on television and in the motion picture theater, and indeed on the covers of many of the slick magazines on sale at the grocery store, that which only a few years ago was considered too vulgar and explicit to be allowed the right to public display. What within my lifetime was considered an affront to the moral dignity and accepted standards of decency is now totally acceptable in any media.

Again, quoting Robert Bork: "There is, of course, more to the case for censorship than the need to preserve a viable democracy. We need also to avoid the social devastation wrought by pornography and endless incitements to murder and mayhem. Whatever the effects upon our capacity to govern ourselves, living in a culture that saturates us with pictures of sex and violence is aesthetically ugly, emotionally flattening, and physically dangerous" (*Slouching Towards Gomorrah,* pp. 142–43).

Twenty-five years ago Dr. Victor Cline, a highly regarded clinical psychologist, authored a book on this issue that he titled, *Where Do You Draw the Line?* The answer to that question is still the critical responsibility of those who for whatever reason are expected to provide the guidance and protection to a generation who must survive the onslaught of degeneracy coming from every conceivable source.

CHAPTER FIVE

"I WANT
TO SEE FILTH"

The title to this chapter comes from a statement made by a woman interviewed by a nationally syndicated columnist as she emerged from an "adult theater." The columnist was attempting to determine why people patronized theaters that showed pornographic films. Most of the patrons declined to be interviewed, and even covered their faces and ran the other way when approached by the columnist. This woman welcomed the interview, but misinterpreted the columnist's purpose as being one of seeking to eliminate the presence of adult theaters in our society. The interviewer's question was whether the female patron felt that the price of the ticket was tantamount to a fraudulent misrepresentation, in that there was no believable story line to the films and nothing remotely close to quality acting.

The woman's response was a defiant confirmation that she found exactly what she expected and what she wanted in the films, and her parting comment was: "I paid for filth and I want to see filth!"

One of the most amazing changes that I have seen in the world of pornography is how the pornographers have now developed a vast market among women. The dramatic change of the last twenty years was brought about through a conscious strategy to make pornography acceptable to women. Proof of their success appears on the covers of a dozen women's magazines: *How To Drive Him Crazy with Desire; How to Cheat on Your Husband; Why Two Lovers are Even Better Than One. . . .*" It goes on and on. What this means is that among other ways in which women are proving that they are equal to men is that they can be equally carnal and sensuous and equally crass in their sexual promiscuity. Above all, they are equally able to bury any instinct for decency if there is enough money involved.

As noted earlier, I am not a clinical psychologist or a practicing psychiatrist. I leave to others the task of analyzing the allure of pornography. "Having a morbid interest in the prurient (i.e., that which excites to lust)" is a phrase frequently contained in judicial opinions related to issues of obscenity. In struggling to develop a coherent legal framework for what constitutes pornography and what does not, the courts have attempted to look behind the material itself to the intent of the publisher or distributor. The motive or intent behind a museum's exhibition of the famed sculpture *Venus de Milo* is not the same as that of the slick magazine publisher or the motion picture producer who presents a bare-breasted woman. As was true with most of the issues involving pornography, the court never did succeed in its quest.

Irrespective of the deeper issues of attraction to and ultimate fascination with the obscene, what is undeniably clear without a degree in psychology or psychiatry is the tragic effect of pornography upon those who become involved in and ultimately addicted to this filth. When people expose themselves to the dirt of pornography, they are quickly infected with an emotional, spiritual, and often physical disease. As their obsession with pornography increases, they soon come to experience various forms of death. They die as to things lovely and virtuous, they die as to their sensitivity and gentleness, they die as to their ability to express affection as opposed to lust and passion. In the ultimate tragedy of pornography they literally bring death into the lives of others.

In an article entitled "Pornography and Callousness" in the *Journal of Communication,* Dr. Dolf Zillman, a professor of communication and psychology at Indiana University, and Dr. Jennings Bryant, a professor of communication and department head at the University of Evansville, reported on an extensive study of the effects of pornography upon those who consumed it. In their study they described as effectively as I have ever seen it done the pathetically deceitful depiction of sex in pornography. They noted:

Most men might disagree with the insinuation that in pornography all sex is rape-like and point to the apparent eagerness on the part of women to do any and everything that holds promise of yielding pleasure. Likewise, many men might take issue with the declaration of ridicule as a purpose and acknowledge a loving preoccupation with basal sexual lust instead. Few would object, however, to the charge of a preponderance of the characterization of women in pornography as anonymous, panting playthings that men liberally exploit for sexual self-gratification and any self-enhancing concomitant thereof.

Indeed, pornography appears to thrive on featuring social encounters in which women are eager to accommodate any and every imaginable sexual urge of about any man in the vicinity. These socially nondiscriminating females are typically shown, in fact, to encourage and actively solicit the specific sexual behaviors that are dear to men, but not necessarily to women. . . . Perhaps most importantly, and presumably a vital part of what has been referred to as "male sexual fantasy," women are portrayed as hysterically euphoric in response to just about any sexual or pseudo-sexual stimulation they receive at the hands of the "male magicians."

Needless to say, sexual reality tends to fall short of such magic. Men, inspired by pornography, may well feel cheated and accuse perfectly sensitive women of frigidity. Lacking corrective information, the women might actually come to doubt themselves—that is, their own sexual sensitivities. Regarding untried activities, pornography again projects euphoria where it might not exist—at least, for many. That pornography thus entices actions, and that the resultant experimentation leads to less than satisfactory results, can hardly be doubted.

Russell (1980) has recently documented that women take the brunt of this type of pornography-inspired experimentation. Men, the aggressively superior gender, were found to have made women comply with their requests to try what had been seen. . . . Requests tended to be backed by brute force, and many women reported feelings of degradation and humiliation in addition to having been hurt physically.

In an incomprehensible chorus of irrationality and lies the defenders of pornography continue to insist that there is no "evidence" that pornography causes antisocial behavior. For years I heard this contention made, often by so-called "experts" with advanced degrees in psychology and psychiatry. Invariably these individuals demonstrated the postulate that not all academics can be considered intellectuals. Others of equal or greater academic and intellectual status would refute and overcome these pathetic assertions with highly skilled studies that documented and confirmed the reality of the negative impact of pornography on the individual who consumes it. That such evidence exists and has existed for more than twenty-five years is continually ignored or dismissed as irrelevant by the minions of publicity-seeking exhibitionists who assert that pornography is "harmless."

The ultra-liberal feminist movement in the United States managed for years to ignore the issue of pornography entirely. The author repeatedly challenged feminist leaders who appeared with him on radio and TV talk shows to explain why their zeal in promoting women's rights did not deal with the most anti-feminist of all activities, pornography. In what has to be one of the most convoluted bits of distorted reasoning of which I am aware, one of the most prominent national leaders of the feminist movement decided to address this failure by attempting to distinguish between "erotica" and "pornography."

Gloria Steinem has been one of the nation's most vocal feminist leaders for nearly three decades. In an article written to "distinguish pornography from erotica" Steinem declared the depiction of "mutually pleasurable sexual expression between people who have enough power to be there by positive choice to constitute 'erotica'; and she endorsed the use of such sensuous stimuli, as they "give us a contagion of pleasure." On the other hand, she condemned as "pornography" any erotic message that features "violence, dominance, and conquest." For erotica to be "erotica," she insisted, portrayals of sex may involve neither a conqueror nor a victim. She was vehement in her rejection of any pornographic attempt at convincing anybody that to women, "pain and humiliation . . . are really the same as pleasure." Again, the "victim-free sexual materials" are given a clean bill of health, and erotica entailing any kind of victimization are not (see "Erotica and Pornography: A Clear and Present Difference," in L. Lederer, ed.; *Take Back the Night: Women on Pornography*, New York: Morrow, 1980).

I have recited the tragedy of Kelly Hulme's being murdered by a man crazed with pornography. Most people are aware of the highly publicized confession of serial rapist and killer Ted Bundy, who in the hour before his execution admitted that he began his spree of depravation and death by becoming addicted to pornography. In Utah during the decade of the eighties five small boys were abducted, sexually abused, and ultimately murdered by a man who also admitted that his total obsession with pornography had propelled him into destroying the lives of these five little boys and bringing unforgettable grief to their families.

During the period of time that I was actively involved as a spokesman for anti-pornography efforts I would invariably find that after speaking to any audience, whether a small group of five or over a thousand, several people would wait after the event was over to share the misery of a family destroyed by pornography. Typical of these agonizing tragedies was the experience of a woman in San Diego, California. When most of the audience had left she came forward and asked for a moment to share her story. It was similar to literally hundreds that I had heard before.

She and her husband had a sweet family of four children. In some way her husband became involved with pornographic material. His intimate behavior toward her changed from an expression of affection and love to one of seeking, and then demanding, participation in forms of sexual behavior totally unnatural and foreign to their marriage. When she refused to participate in his requests he became physically violent and abusive. One day he stormed out of the home and left for several days.

She later learned that he had driven to Nevada and spent hundreds of dollars in buying the sexual perversions that the pornography had implanted into his mind. The double tragedy evolved that he found nothing of the anticipated and promised pleasures in these experiences which the deceit of pornography had led him to anticipate, but he could not extricate himself from the emotional muck into which he had willingly immersed himself. The marriage ended in divorce as another family suffered the agonizing harvest of the pornographer's fare.

Frequently I was asked by a deeply embarrassed and distraught wife if I could recommend a professional therapist who might assist her in bringing her husband back to reality insofar as their personal intimacy was concerned. Only the most intense agony of soul could lead these women to approach someone they had never before seen or heard to plead for guidance in finding a way to restore a loved one who had become lost to them in the world of pornography.

There are thousands of documented cases of pornography leading to ruined lives, often including the vicious attack by the pornography addict on another human being. In 1972 I received the following letter from a noted clinical psychologist at the University of Utah, Victor B. Cline, Ph.D. Following is his letter:

> Dear Senator Harmer:
>
> I understand that you wished some "case history" type data on how exposure to pornography might have harmful or antisocial effects on people. Let me cite several cases from my files.
>
> A young LDS girl, age 13, became pregnant, when she discovered the secret hiding place of pornography in her home . . . and "tried out" with a neighboring 14-year-old boy what they saw in the pictures. This went on for six months . . . before they were found out by the girl's pregnancy.
>
> A young married couple came in for marriage counseling because the husband was addicted to pornography in triple X movies. He weekly went to these movies for sexual arousal and practiced masturbation in the theatre for release. This later spread to use or addiction to pornographic books where the same thing occurred. Sexual relations in marriage was sharply curtailed, the wife felt very rejected because she felt her husband felt more attracted to what he read in a book or saw on the screen than for her as his living caring wife. Acute marital problems ensued. The man was an active elder in the (LDS) church. There are a number of instances of this type case.
>
> A young unmarried 18-year-old priest (LDS) found himself caught up in a pattern of addiction to the triple X type movie and masturbation with ensuing feelings of guilt, lack of self-worth, and inability to control the habit. This interfered with being called on a mission.
>
> A vice squad police officer (in a Western city, non-LDS) brought pornography home that he confiscated in his line of work. It was first used to add excitement to marital relationships, but later daughters became involved. It wrecked the marriage and the family.

Older homosexual exposed teen age Mormon boy to pornography to sexually excite and turn him on as part of seduction of boy into homosexual activities.

If these very brief synopses of case histories which I am personally familiar with in my professional work illustrate the problem for you well enough please use them at your discretion.

Yours sincerely,

Victor B. Cline, Ph.D

From the thousands of similar authoritative statements I have selected just one more example: "Antisocial, delinquent, and criminal activity frequently result from sexual stimulation by pornography. This abnormal sexual stimulation creates such a demand for expression that gratification by vicarious means follows. Girls run away from their homes and become entangled in prostitution. Boys and young men have difficulty resisting the undue sexual stimulation, become sexually aggressive and generally incorrigible" (Dr. Nicholas G. Frignito, Chief Psychiatrist, Philadelphia Municipal Court).

I return to a theme that is presented repeatedly throughout this book, which is that what was clearly considered to be pornography less than thirty years ago is now acceptable as "family entertainment" (i.e., PG-13 rated movies). In chapter 3 I quoted from an article by LDS film producer Kieth Merrill that appeared in the March 21, 1998 issue of the *Deseret News*. In that same article Merrill quotes the review given to one of the so-called PG-13 movies that he warns is anything but family-worthy entertainment. The review, written by a non-LDS reviewer, notes as follows regarding the film "In & Out," rated PG-13: "The most accurate review of the film I've read comes from Movieguide presented by Ted Baehr. They called it 'Sneak Attack.' "

The noted review is then quoted by Merrill: "Strong homosexual worldview to promote homosexuality, rebuke homophobia and normalize a politically correct agenda. It includes obscenities, profanity, strong homosexual innuendo with graphic descriptions, sexual humor and one homosexual kiss, upper male nudity, alcohol use, smoking and lying. 'In & Out' is not a movie for those who hold that sexual relations are a sacred gift from God."

Query: How many "active LDS youth" went to see this PG-13 motion picture because it was not R rated? How does one measure the loss of spiritual light and virtue that the viewing of this obscene film brought into their lives?

During the mid-1990s ample evidence was found to prove that the tobacco industry had known for years the addictive and cancer-causing attributes of nicotine. Some cigarette manufacturers were proven to have actually added stronger addictive substances to the tobacco in their cigarettes in order to intensify the dependency of the smoker upon the tobacco. Yet for decades the tobacco industry has contended—with myriad scientific reports created by highly credentialed medical doctors—that none of these things were true. The blatancy of this duplicity has finally brought about some modest demands for punishment of the tobacco industry.

Even more duplicitous and deceitful has been the continued assertion by the allies of the pornographer—the Motion Picture Association of America, the ACLU, and the slick magazine publishers—that pornography is neither harmful nor is there any evidence that pornography has any causal relationship to antisocial behavior. The parents of those thousands of boys and girls who have been raped, tortured, and in many cases murdered by individuals addicted to and crazed by pornography are not to be considered as "reliable" witnesses concerning what tragedy inevitably follows the pornography addict's path into degeneracy.

In the last forty years there have been literally thousands of credible studies reported that have confirmed the reality that continued exposure to pornography produces violent antisocial behavior. The evidence is so overwhelming that it is beyond rational explanation as to why any society would continue to tolerate the presence of such an obvious source of destructive forces. Yet pornography is not only tolerated but also is actively defended by the naive librarians, the neurotic academician who is obsessed with the need for some type of recognition, the contemptuous lawyers whose integrity and honor were dissolved long ago in their pursuit of fame and fortune, and above all, the motion picture producers who reap such enormous profits from a society becoming more and more desensitized to evil and degeneracy. The pornographers themselves have no need to make any defense of their vile craft. Others stand all too ready to do so.

The most compelling evidence of the causal relationship between pornography and violent sexual abuse of women and children comes from the law enforcement officers, who continually find that the perpetrators of these crimes are overwhelmingly pornography addicts. What is most distressing, however, is that it now appears certain that the majority of these crimes of rape, child abuse, physical torture associated with unlawful sexual behavior, and so on, are never reported. The victims, for a variety of reasons, prefer to be spared the further emotional trauma and agony of reliving the event. There is an avalanche of emerging data regarding wives and children of men addicted to pornography being subjected to hideous and indescribably vile abuse from husbands and fathers. Most of these victims never report their suffering to law enforcement officials.

Anyone interested in obtaining copies of these very credible scientific studies on the effect of pornography might contact the National Coalition Against Pornography at 800 Compton Road, Suite 9224, Cincinnati, Ohio, 45231. In fact a variety of honorable organizations throughout the country will make available very valid data on the effect of pornography. The office of the National Coalition Against Pornography will gladly provide the names and addresses of other such organizations.

Following is a sampling of a summary of studies on "Pornography's Relationship to Abnormal Sexual Behavior/Sexual Offenders" as compiled by M. Douglas Reed in 1989, and as provided in one compilation prepared by the National Coalition Against Pornography noted above. The italic type heading in each case refers to the author or title of the study.

David A. Scott (1985)

Pornography can lead to sexual deviancy for disturbed and normal people alike; pornography is addictive (see Victor Cline); pornography is the literature of sexual deviants (paraphiliacs). Users of pornography frequently lose faith in the viability of marriage.

Abel, et al (1987)

The frequency of self-reported crimes [for the non-incarcerated sex offenders studied] was vastly greater than the number of crimes for which they had been arrested.

The ratio of arrest to commission of the more violent crimes such as rape and child molestation was approximately 1:30. In terms of the less aggressive crimes . . . only 1 in 150 deviant sexual episodes actually led to arrest.

Dietz and Sears (1988)

Much pornography pairs violent, degrading, humiliating, or other (perhaps aversive) deviant images with more ordinary sexual stimuli that are arousing despite rather than because of the simultaneous presence of the deviant image.

This pairing of unconditioned sexual stimuli (stimuli that elicit natural or unconditioned responses) with violent, degrading, humiliating, and deviant sexual images can play an important role in the development and maintenance of paraphilias (sexual deviations). . . . The content of pornography to which cohorts of boys—or boys as a group are repeatedly exposed, at least during the critical developmental period around puberty, shapes the distribution of sexual deviations that the cohort or group will manifest as its members reach adulthood. . . . Obscene materials play a role in creating new and enduring unhealthy and unwholesome—i.e., prurient—interests.

Marshall (1983)

He found that 86% of rapists admitted regular use of pornography, with 57% admitting actual imitation of pornography scenes in commission of sex crimes.

Victor Cline, Ph.D. (Utah Psychologist)

He identified a common pattern of progression with many pornography users (sex offenders):

(1) addiction to hard core pornography;

(2) escalation in the need for more shocking material;

(3) desensitization toward initially shocking material; and

(4) an increased tendency to "act out" sexual activities seen in pornography.

Dolf Zillman and Jennings Bryant

Massive exposure to pornography produced persisting impressions of hypersexuality in society and prompted liberal attitudes concerning the dissemination of pornography. Most significantly, it fostered callousness toward women and trivialized rape as a criminal offense ("Effects of Massive Exposure to Pornography" in Neil M. Malamuth & Edward Donnerstein, ed., *Pornography And Sexual Aggression,* Orlando: Academic Press, 1984).

From the thousands of valid studies that have been carried out and reported regarding the correlation between the ingesting of pornography and antisocial deviant behavior, two critical themes constantly emerge. The first is, that the appetite for pornography becomes an addiction of dependency upon having pornography that is increasingly more deviant, more vile, more violent, more abusive and degenerate. The second is, that as the assimilation of pornography continues, the desensitization of the individual to what would ordinarily be totally abhorrent becomes so pronounced that every normal inhibition against deviant behavior ultimately disappears. Thus we have the recorded instances of pornography-addicted individuals committing crimes of such a hideous nature in the violence and abuse of another human being that many refuse to believe that one human being could or would actually do such things to another human being.

An example of this progression can be seen in the results of a thirty-year study of the content of the best known of the so-called "soft-core" pornographic publications, *Playboy* magazine. The following study was reported by Judith A. Reismann, Ph.D., and contained in a study prepared for The Ontario Human Rights Commission, entitled *"Pornography in Neighborhood Convenience Stores: Neurochemical Effects on Women."* The study was published by The Institute for Media Education, Box 7404, Arlington, Va., 22207, as revised January 18, 1993. Quoting from the study:

> In *Making Violence Sexy: Feminist Views on Pornography,* (1993, ed. D. Russell) feminist theoreticians, Andrea Dworkin and Catherine MacKinnon, describe the discriminatory role of *Playboy* in establishing a stressful threatening environment for women as "less than human," as legitimate "bunny" prey to be hunted. The authors note that: *"Playboy,* in both text and pictures, promotes rape . . . and child sexual abuse . . .

(making) a specialty of targeting women for sexual harassment: working women, including nurses, police, and military personnel: and presumptively educated women, including university students and lawyers. . . . The women in *Playboy* are presented in postures of submission . . . as sexual objects and commodities" (p.79).

Some fourteen years earlier, Dr. Reo Christenson wrote an insightful and indicting summary of another one of the widely distributed pornographic slick magazines as follows: "Its message is that sex is divorced from love, commitment, morality and responsibility; that it is a purely animal act, no more and no less; that it is unrelated to privacy; that deviant sex is the most adventurous and exciting sex; that women's importance is to be found in their genital organs which are fair game for whoever wishes to exploit them; that irresponsible sex has no consequences—no venereal disease, unwanted pregnancies, abortions, premature marriages, psychic traumas. Some message" (Dr. Reo Christenson, *The Judgment of Hustler, Sanity, Not Censorship,* Cincinnati Enquirer, February 11, 1979).

Apologists for the pornographers have another favorite ploy. They talk about "victimless crimes" as though there were such a thing, especially in the muck of pornography. Pornography is so obviously harmful, and yet there are those of high academic reputation or political power who blatantly refuse to admit the truth no matter how strong the evidence.

The inconsistency of the assertions made by these apologists for the pornographers is blatantly obvious. Their constant series of lies is reminiscent of the tobacco industry's constant assertion that the use of tobacco had "no causal relationship to becoming afflicted with cancer." So it is with the relationship of pornography and violence, as exhibited on television and the motion picture screen, to human behavior. A well-known liberal columnist, Nicholas van Hoffman, wrote as follows:

Why is it that liberals who believe "role models" in third grade readers are of decisive influence on behavior when it concerns racism or male chauvinist piggery, laugh at the assertion that pornography may also teach rape? Every textbook in every public school system in the nation has been overhauled in the last twenty years because it was thought that the blond, blue-eyed urban children once depicted therein taught little people a socially dangerous ethnocentrism. If textbooks, those vapid and insipid instruments of such slight influence, can have had such sweeping effect, what are we to surmise about the effects on the impressionably young of an R or X-rated movie, in wide-screen technicolor, with Dolby sound and every device of cinematic realism?

Network television executives who deny the likelihood their programs can alter human behavior lie, and they know it. All you have to do is listen to what these same gentlemen say to their advertisers. They boast, they brag, they bellow about what an effective sales medium their networks are . . . how good they are at getting people to alter their behavior and part with their money. ("Assault by Film," *Washington Post,* 13 April 1979, p. D-4)

Through the past twenty years the evidence on violence, the clinical, psychologically professionally developed evidence, continues to mount. But in structure (and often in practice) what happens in the human mind and consciousness—and unconsciousness—when sex is depicted is no different from what happens when violence is depicted. Two things happen: (1) many impressionable viewers do act out what they have seen; (2) all of the viewers are left with lasting impressions that sink into the subconscious mind, and if frequent enough (and for some persons, even if not frequent) these impressions influence and warp their entire attitude about life and about other human beings. As Dr. Frederick Wertham put it:

> Negative media effects do not generally consist in simple imitation. They are indirect, long range, and cumulative. Violent images are stored in the brain, and if, when and how they are retrieved depends on many circumstances. It is a question not so much of acts as of attitudes, not of specific deeds but of personality developments. . . .
>
> The saturation of people's minds with brutal and cruel images can have a long-range influence on their emotional life. It is an effect that involves human relations in fantasy and in fact and can become a contributing factor to emotional troubles and adjustment difficulties. . . .
>
> With regard to sex, the explicit display of sadomasochistic scenes may have lasting effects. They may supply the first suggestions for special forms of deviancy or reinforce existing tendencies. The whole ori-

entation of young people with regard to the dignity of women is affected. By showing cruelty with erotic overtones, we teach that there can be pleasure in inflicting pain on others. ("Medicine and Mayhem," *M.D. Magazine,* June 1978, p. 11)

The incredible power of the Internet has now brought hard-core pornography into the reach of every home. It is amazing that those who acknowledge the need to deal with pornography on the Internet have fallen into the same trap that the pornographers so successfully baited in the past, the trap of attempting to separate children from adults as regards the capacity of pornography to destroy lives. With all of the talk about protecting children from pornography on the Internet we lose sight of the reality that you cannot protect children from pornography if you do not also protect adults from pornography. We cannot stop child pornography if we do not stop the adult pornographers.

The idea that we can isolate children from Internet pornography and still allow it to exist for adults is as naive as believing that it would be possible to insulate or quarantine children from a contagious pestilence but permit adults to breathe freely the germs and contaminants that blow about in polluted air. Pornography on the Internet is an education system. It teaches. Its message is: human beings are mere animals; the highest value is immediate pleasure; other people may be used and then discarded.

The content and nature of women's magazines now on the newsstand also show the incredible degree to which they are contributing to the increased acceptance of pornography among women. There are now a dozen or more such magazines, written by and for women, in which the predominant theme is sexual ecstacy. The articles in these magazines depict the ease with which women may discard sexual inhibitions and find "fulfillment" (a term that pornographers have used and abused for decades) in their newfound sexual freedom. The effect of this incredible slide into the mire has been to hasten the time when these readers will require more and more explicit sexual materials to satisfy their newfound appetite for the obscene.

Only the most naive could believe that this sequence is coincidental. It is not. There is a very active correlation between what the "legitimate" media depicts and promotes as acceptable behavior and what the pornographers initially present as "normal love-making." The process is ever ongoing in both the printed and motion picture media. The inevitable result and overt purpose is to create an ever-increasing appetite for the obscene, which as it becomes more graphic also becomes more expensive. As we noted earlier, a pornographic product never becomes obsolete, it has no shelf life, and thus the ultimate profitability of producing pornography is ever assured.

I noted in chapter 2 the decisions of the United States Supreme Court that became the burden of proof that a prosecutor had to meet in seeking a conviction against a pornographer. One of the key elements of the burden of proof was that the offending material "was patently offensive and violated contemporary local community standards of decency." The prosecutor had the burden of establishing what the "contemporary community standards" were for the local community. It became one of the more difficult aspects of the burden of proof upon the prosecution.

In May of 1989 a Los Angeles Superior Court judge dismissed complaints against four pornographic films because "he could not conclude that the films were patently offensive in an area as diverse as Los Angeles" (*Los Angeles Times,* Thursday, May 4, 1989). The four films included graphic depictions of group sex, oral sex, beatings and bondage, gang rape, and a woman committing suicide after she had been sexually attacked. "I cannot say beyond a reasonable doubt that community standards were violated," stated the judge.

The majority of the nation's pornography producers and distributors (except those on the Internet) are located in Los Angeles. A decision like the one noted above essentially says that there is no way under the current Supreme Court guidelines to find that pornographic material, no matter how vile, degenerate, and violent, actually goes beyond the local community standard of decency.

We noted earlier that the academic community in the last ten years has come to embrace the subject of pornography as proper classroom material. Deservedly obscure academics who have no other way to distinguish themselves have achieved their goal of fame by virtue of promoting the "study" of pornographic materials and their "effect" upon men, women, and even children. In August of

1998 this curriculum of so-called higher education descended to the ultimate depths with the sponsorship by the California State University at Northridge of the "World Conference on Pornography."

For three days the conference presented an unending stream of hard-core pornography, all under the guise of "academic analysis." The conference presented awards to the producers of hard-core pornography films, to the actors and actresses of the same, and to the various exhibitors who have "pioneered" the introduction of hardcore pornography throughout the world. The organizers of the conference, with the hypocrisy that can only come from people of this degenerate nature, stated disingenuously that "while the organizers do not agree with all of the various positions that may be presented, we strongly endorse the right of presentation and discussion."

The conference presented an award to one of the California attorneys who has made a fortune defending hard-core pornography in the courtroom. The keynote address was given by (who else but?) the president of the National ACLU, Nadine Strossen. Displayed at the conference was every form of hard-core pornography that has been produced, from comic books to expensive motion pictures, from amateur home videos of excretion and sexual perversion to specialized highly professional videocassettes produced for homosexuals and lesbians.

The national president of the ACLU, Nadine Strossen, spoke with pride over the fact that the lawsuit that killed the Communications Decency Act bears the name *Reno v. ACLU*. The Communications Decency Act was the initial attempt by Congress to restrict the transmission of pornography over the Internet. The ACLU immediately earned their financial support from the MPAA and the pornography industry by filing a lawsuit against the act.

Strossen is an appropriate individual to head the ACLU. Her book, *Defending Pornography: Free Speech, Sex and the Fight for Women's Rights,* presents all of the predictable arguments for the unrestricted distribution of obscenity. She typifies the feminist hatred of the traditional family unit and the role of the husband and the father in providing for and being responsible for the welfare of the family.

In a press interview given after her speech the ACLU's national

president noted sadly that the one Internet obscenity case the ACLU
lost was on the issue of community standards. The court in that case
held that the "community standards" need not be extended to cover
the entire nation. Having a "standard of decency" that covered the
entire nation would mean reducing every community standard to the
lowest in the country (possibly Los Angeles), which is what the
ACLU wanted, since it would be impossible for a local prosecutor to
quantify the standards as part of the burden of proof in an obscenity
prosecution. One can understand now Judge Robert Bork's comment:
"The head of the ACLU announced in a panel discussion that the
Supreme Court's failure to throw protection around nude dancing in
night clubs was a terrible blow to our freedom of speech. Some years
back, when I suggested to a law school audience that the courts had
gone too far in preventing communities from prohibiting pornography, the then president of the organization (ACLU) compared me
to Salazar of Portugal and the Greek Colonels. Afterward he said he
had called me a fascist. It is fascinating that when one calls for
greater democratic control and less governance by a judicial oli-
garchy, one is immediately called a fascist. The ACLU seems to think
democracy is tyranny and government by judges is freedom" (Robert
Bork, *Slouching Towards Gomorrah,* [New York: Regan Books,
1996], p. 153).

Among the most stunning aspects of an event that could only be
described as "beyond comprehension" were the number of women
faculty members who actively participated, and the significant
amount of pornographic material being produced by women for
women. The conference left no doubt that in the United States
women have become more than equal with men as they have aggressively entered into the production and distribution of pornography.

Given the presentation of this conference in Los Angeles, could
any judge or jury ever again assert that a pornographic item could be
found to be "patently offensive to the moral standards of the local
community"? Hardly.

Ninety-nine point ninety-nine percent of human beings recoil at
the sight of a venomous serpent. The initial reaction to pornography
is usually the same, one of disgust and revulsion at the sight of something so abhorrent. But as darkness replaces light the allure of

pornography grows. Unlike the venomous serpent, but very much like the constrictor, pornography slowly wraps it coils around each victim until escape is no longer possible. Death, always spiritual, almost always emotional, and sometimes physical, is the inevitable result.

CHAPTER SIX

A CALIFORNIA
BALLOT INITIATIVE

—————

By 1971 Clancy, Schulzke, and I had had enough experience in the courts that we were determined to develop some legislation that would give local prosecutors the ability to effectively fight against the production and distribution of pornographic materials in their communities. We spent several months preparing the legislation and introduced it into the California state senate in a package of bills in 1971 and 1972. We knew that the opposition would come from the motion picture industry, the slick magazine producers and distributors, and the pornographers themselves. Always the visible spokesmen for the opposition would be led by their hostage minions in the ACLU. The people who run these entities didn't organize all of those high society fund-raisers for the ACLU out of a sense of love for the Constitution. They had paid a lot of money for the ACLU's charade support, and they never failed to collect.

Collect they did. Notwithstanding my position as the Republican caucus chairman in the Senate, and my personal friendship with many members of the opposite political party in both houses of the legislature, the failure in our fight for passage of these bills was one of the bitterest defeats of my political career. The pattern before the committees was invariably the same. I could recite the condescending litany from memory. The blatant hypocrisy and maliciousness of it all was what made it especially bitter.

"We commend Senator Harmer for his good intentions," they would say, barely concealing their contempt for our efforts. "As much as we agree with him that the presence of pornographic material in our communities is a tragic blight, if these bills are allowed to become law they will most certainly have violated well-established Constitutional principles associated with the First Amendment. The enactment of these bills will allow fanatic zealots to suppress freedom of speech and many acknowledged literary masterpieces."

Then would follow a chorus of witnesses carefully selected from among law school faculties and community groups (particularly odious were the librarians who were an easily duped into fronting for these people), each able to detail the inevitable destruction of great literary classics in the equivalent of what would be book burning if our legislation were adopted. It was so nauseating because of the arrogant duplicity that was involved. But it was devastatingly effective.

We had presented a carefully researched presentation by prosecutors who outlined the scope of the problem involving the sale and distribution of pornography in their communities and the immense difficulty of fighting it without the statutory enactments we were presenting. Highly prestigious legal authorities testified that the proposed statutes certainly did meet the constitutional requirements of the First Amendment and the decisions of the Supreme Court. We presented various case histories of tragedies similar to those of Kelly Hulme and hundreds of other innocent victims of the evil of pornography. Reluctantly, but knowing we had no choice, we presented to the committees examples of the materials we were seeking to suppress, both in motion picture and slick magazine. We presented the testimony of highly competent psychiatrists and psychologists regarding the devastating effect on marriages and in individual lives as the addiction to pornography took hold.

One of the bills that I was confident could not be defeated was Senate Bill 699 (1972 session), which related to the rapidly increasing use of young children in pornographic materials. Over the prior ten years the use of children or young teenagers in pornographic materials had increased dramatically. Our bill specified that anyone who produced or distributed such materials that were found by the court (a jury of local citizens) to be "intended or designed to appeal to the sexual curiosity or the prurient interest of the purchaser" was guilty of a misdemeanor. We resisted the desire to make the crime a felony, even though it surely deservcd to be, simply to avoid the opposition's predictable hysteria over the idea that someone could actually be sent to prison as a felon for exploiting children for sexually deviant purposes.

The bill did make it through the senate but was defeated in the assembly by the same cadre of opponents noted above. The speciousness and hypocrisy of their presentations were so blatant and so contemptuous of the issues involved that in my own mind those who made the presentations somehow reached depths of darkness that even the pornographers had not been able to achieve.

A companion bill (Senate Bill 698) related to the exhibition of such materials to minors. It suffered the same fate.

Senate Bill 1473 of the 1972 session defined "obscene" and "prurient interest" in accordance with the latest pronouncements of the Supreme Court. The bill also set forth certain changes in the Penal Code relating to the crimes of production and distribution of obscene matter. The other bills in the group included Senate Bill 1208, which gave the prosecutors the ability to seek injunctive relief from the court to stop the exhibition of an obscene presentation until the issue was resolved in the court. The prosecutors needed this tool because often the pornographers would simply use delaying tactics in the court process while they continued to exhibit or sell the offending material. By the time the court did act, even in the rare instances when the prosecution prevailed, the pornographer would have completed exhibiting the film or selling the magazine that was the subject of the complaint, and the prosecutor would have to start all over again using a new film or publication.

A proposed amendment to the state constitution was intended to give local communities much greater ability to apply the "contemporary standards" of decency within that community when the issue of those standards with regard to the prosecution of obscene material was involved.

Senate Bill 701 addressed the issue of the rapidly increasing presentation of sadomasochistic abuse in pornographic materials. Sadomasochism is the combination of physical abuse, torture, flagellation, or similar conduct with patently sexually deviant material. Like the pedophelia referred to above, the incidence of this type of material in pornography was increasing at such a substantial rate that its vileness and debauchery were becoming indescribably degenerate.

At the same time that I was involved in the anti-pornography movement I was the vice chairman of the California State Senate Committee on Education. A great deal of my time was spent in dealing with many of the serious problems involving the quality of instruction in the public schools of California. I was also recognized as one of the emerging authorities on higher education in the state. In 1968 I had published a book on the problems of education and welfare in California that Governor Ronald Reagan had personally distributed to his state cabinet members and other appointed officials with a strong recommendation that they read it.

Since I had these credentials in the area of education it was natural that those individuals and groups who were concerned with the emergence of very graphic materials in so-called "sex education" classes should appeal to me for assistance. It was in fact true that the "fad" of sex education classes was spreading rapidly throughout the state, and often exhibitionist teachers were presenting very graphic materials to fifth- and sixth-grade classes.

After carefully examining the materials involved and confirming the allegations that these materials were being presented to eleven- and twelve-year-old students I did give my support to the efforts being made to put much stricter controls on the use and content of such materials. I sponsored appropriate legislation in the senate and exercised my influence with the Education Committee in a variety of ways that significantly assisted in halting the momentum of the spread of these materials. One of the expert witnesses (a psychiatrist who specialized in dealing with neurotic children) who testified in support of one of these bills in the Education Committee commented that the effect of these "sex education" materials was analogous to "teaching a goose to fly south. The problem was," he said, " the goose ended up flying south in the middle of the summer instead of in the fall."

Because of my concurrent efforts involving pornography and the abuse of sex education in the schools, the opponents to my package of bills about pornography were able to initiate an effective smear campaign involving my personal life and my family. Keeping these malicious lies away from my wife and my children became impossible, and their distress at knowing these things were appearing in the press and being spoken in public became a heavy personal burden as I dealt with the problems of pornography.

By late April of 1972 it was obvious that the financial power of the pornographers would make it impossible for my colleagues and me to succeed in the legislature. Although I would continue my legislative efforts as long as there was any hope of success (meaning until the bills were actually defeated in committee or by a floor vote), I determined to initiate an alternative to the legislative process.

The California constitution (as do many other state constitutions) provides that under certain conditions the people themselves may enact statutory provisions or make changes to the state constitution when the legislature will not do so. Usually these conditions involve obtaining a certain minimum number of signatures of duly registered voters on petitions that contain the proposed statutory language. These petitions need to be presented to the chief election officer of the state (usually the secretary of state) who, after validating the signatures as being those of registered voters, will then place the proposed statute on the next ballot.

In 1972 in California, with one-tenth of the entire American population living within the state, an initiative petition would have to obtain over one million valid signatures in order to qualify for the ballot. The usual ratio of valid to invalid signatures was two to one, meaning that it was necessary to get three signatures in order to get two signatures of properly registered voters. The time ordinarily required to collect a sufficient number of valid signatures was eight months to a year, or even longer. The cost usually came to about a dollar per signature.

In order to submit to the county clerks and the secretary of state sufficient signatures for the November ballot, all of the petitions bearing signatures would have to be submitted by the middle of June. That would give the county clerks and the secretary of state sufficient time to validate the signatures.

In other words, in mid-April there were slightly more than eight weeks remaining from the time I conceived the idea of submitting the anti-pornography statutes to the voters to the time in mid-June when the petitions bearing the signatures would have to be submitted to the proper officials. Logistically it would require a full-time staff of twenty or thirty paid people, plus several thousand paid petition circulators, to accomplish such a task. The cost would be several million dollars even if all of the other logistical challenges could be resolved.

At this time the chief of staff in my senate office was a brilliant young man from San Diego, Bill Price. Bill was a graduate of Brigham Young University with a master's degree in public administration. He was a consummately skillful organizer and administrator. Hard working but ever cheerful, Bill was the perfect person to direct a staff which at that time included a dozen people on my senate staff and another eight or ten individuals who were on my caucus chairman staff.

I put Bill to work on the logistics for organizing a statewide effort to circulate petitions on a door-to-door basis. Traditionally most petitions were circulated by the sponsor's paid professional signature collectors, who would set up a table in a shopping mall or similar place of heavy pedestrian traffic and would then appeal to anyone passing by to sign the petition (as a registered voter) and to provide his or her correct address. For the county clerks that made the verification process very tedious, because each signature, with an address, had to be located and confirmed on the rolls of the voters. Since the people signing the petitions came from every possible direction there was no continuity of names and addresses in the verification process.

My assignment to Bill Price was to develop a strategy that would have the petition circulators go from door to door. This would make the gathering of the signatures more efficient and, above all, make the verification process more certain. Since we had to gather signatures from every county in the state, we must have someone in each county—or in the larger counties someone in each legislative district—responsible to coordinate the effort and deliver the petitions to the county clerk. Within two days Bill had the entire process reduced to paper with every task and assignment clearly outlined.

I assigned Ernie Schulzke to take our legislative bills and reduce them to a single cohesive statutory provision that could be printed on a petition. Before we could do anything else we had to be able to submit the petitions to the office of the attorney general for approval or correction. If the proposed initiative measure was not properly drafted the attorney general would have to return it for corrections until it was prepared in a manner acceptable to be submitted to the voters. That process could take more than a month. We would have no time for second chances, so Ernie's drafting had to be correctly accomplished in the next forty-eight hours.

I telephoned the attorney general and told him that I was sending over the draft of an initiative petition to be submitted to the voters on the November ballot, and I needed it to be given the highest priority so that we could get it approved and the petitions printed. He paused for a moment, and then his response was, "You mean the November ballot in 1974."

"No," I responded, "I mean the November ballot this year."

"Senator," he said, "you would have eight weeks to gather the signatures and get them to the county clerks for verification. There is no way you could make that happen in the time you have. Your first opportunity will be the June ballot in 1974."

I finally made him understand that I fully expected to accomplish all of this in the eight weeks remaining, and that the proposed initiative measure would be hand delivered to his office within forty-eight hours. He was obviously irritated at my insistence on pursuing the impossible, but he promised to have his staff immediately review the draft language for any errors or required changes and get it back to me with his approval letter.

Applying his usual intensity of effort Ernie Schulzke produced a document that needed no correction or modification in order to meet the requirements for proper statutory drafting. Within forty-eight hours of the time the attorney general's office received Ernie's draft it was back on my desk with the required letter from the attorney general approving the language as being properly prepared for submission to the voters.

While Bill Price and Ernie Schulzke were performing their assignments I undertook what would be the most difficult of all aspects of the strategy. In reality there was only one way that over a million signatures of registered voters could be collected within this period of time. That would require mobilizing the assistance of thousands of members of the Church through the state.

Just after my initial election to the senate in 1966 I was given an opportunity to meet Elder Howard W. Hunter of the Quorum of the Twelve Apostles of The Church of Jesus Christ of Latter-day Saints. Elder Hunter came from Pasadena, California, and was the member of the Quorum who was responsible for public affairs issues in California. On several occasions he and I had met to discuss matters of public policy that were of concern to the Church. We had frequently corresponded on many of these issues. Of great concern to the Church was the rapidly increasing incidence of the production and distribution of pornographic materials.

I telephoned Elder Hunter and explained the entire situation, the original pieces of legislation, the opposition's ability to undermine my efforts with other legislators, and the concept of taking the issue directly to the voters. Then I got directly to the point. If the local Church leaders could be given the authority to allow us to call upon volunteers from among the members of the Church in their local units to assist us in circulating the petitions it might be possible to put the proposed statutes on the November ballot.

After listening to my proposal, Elder Hunter paused for several moments, and then he said, "Put all of this into a concise letter and get it to me as soon as possible. As soon as I have your letter I will take it to the First Presidency." The letter was written and sent by courier to Salt Lake City so that it was on his desk the next day.

Several days passed during which we pressed forward with organizing the drive to gather the signatures. When the attorney general sent back the draft of the initiative with his signature we immediately took it to the printer. I used three thousand dollars of funds gathered for my re-election campaign to print the petitions. Even giving the matter an immediate priority, it was going to take the printer the better part of a week to get fifty thousand copies of the petitions printed. Each petition had to contain all of the language of the proposed statute along with twenty-five lines for names and addresses of registered voters to sign the petition.

On Thursday afternoon I was engaged in a debate on the floor of the senate when my secretary came to inform me that Elder Hunter was "holding on the telephone waiting to talk to [me]." I immediately went to the telephone booth with my heart pounding at a dramatically increased rate. Unless this phone call contained an unprecedented and literally miraculous approval of my request, everything else we had struggled to accomplish would be in vain.

Elder Hunter got right to the point. He had just left a meeting of the entire First Presidency and the Council of the Twelve Apostles, where my letter was read and discussed at great length. The First Presidency had decided to approve my request. A letter would be prepared and sent out the next day to all Regional Representatives, stake presidents, and bishops in California, in which the First Presidency would be endorsing my effort and asking that local members be encouraged to give whatever assistance possible in circulating the petitions. So overwhelming was the spiritual and emotional impact of Elder Hunter's phone call that after he had hung up I had to remain for several minutes in the privacy of the phone booth in order to regain my composure.

We did not wait for the letter from the First Presidency to arrive before beginning our organizing efforts. I began to make immediate telephone contact with Regional Representatives and stake presidents whom I knew would accept my word regarding the coming letter and its content. In fact the letter did arrive throughout the state the following Tuesday, and our first meetings began the next evening.

Within a few days after that we had organized ourselves so that we could hold three or four meetings a night. The meetings all took place in the LDS chapels throughout the state. The usual format was that I would arrive with several individuals who would be responsible for coordinating the petition circulating efforts in that geographic area. I would give a fifteen- to twenty-minute talk explaining the purpose of the petition drive and the process to be followed. Then the local area maps we had brought with us would be laid out and assignments made for circulating petitions in that community.

It was pleasantly humorous to watch the reaction of those who were not members of the Church who came with me to these meetings. The maps we brought were divided into political precincts, which is the normal way a campaign of this type would be organized. The local LDS members would immediately redraw the maps with ward and stake boundaries and then make their assignments. Within a few minutes the entire area to be covered had been assigned to various volunteers, who then took their petitions and maps and went on their way. My non-LDS associates (political activists whom I had recruited and hired to coordinate the effort on a county-wide basis) would stand in awe at the way in which the LDS volunteers organized themselves, accepted their assignments, developed their own administrative structure from top to bottom, and were on their way to circulate the petitions, all in less than an hour.

It should be noted that not every local LDS leader was willing to help or interested in participating in the project. However, those who declined to assist were few in number and their lack of support did not materially hamper our efforts. Because of the letter from the First Presidency the vast majority of all of the local ecclesiastical leaders were very supportive. It was stunning to watch the efficiency and power with which the existing organization of the Church was able to grasp the challenge and move dramatically to accomplish the task.

Once we developed the routine of the meetings we scheduled three or four meetings a night in which we could meet with several hundred volunteers. For three weeks straight I would be in the state capitol throughout the day and then in some part of the state that night holding organizational meetings. At that time I owned and flew my own airplane, which made it possible to get anywhere from the Oregon border to the southernmost portions of the state to hold our meetings. Often it was well past midnight when we returned to land at Sacramento, but the excitement of possibly dealing such a vital blow for truth and virtue energized us beyond anything we had previously experienced.

When I began receiving telephone calls from county clerks around the state regarding the quality of the petitions being submitted to their offices, I knew that we would achieve our goal. The county clerks would call to congratulate me on the quality of the petitions they were receiving. By going door to door our volunteers had made the verification process so much easier that it required only one-tenth of the time that petition signature verification usually required. The clerks were uniformly amazed at the quality and the quantity of the petitions arriving. They in turn were able to certify the results to the secretary of state in record time. By the end of the second week of

June the county clerks had forwarded to the secretary of state more than sufficient signatures to qualify us for the November ballot, and we still had petitions coming in.

The secretary of state contacted me some three days before our mid-June deadline to inform me that he had formally certified our initiative measure for the ballot, and had assigned to us the designation of "Ballot Proposition 18." For the next five months, "Prop. 18," as we called it, totally dominated my every thought and act. Somehow in the midst of all that effort in other parts of the state my own constituents in the twenty-first senatorial district still re-elected me with a very substantial margin of victory.

To say that others were amazed at what we had accomplished in so short a period of time and with literally no funds available would be an incredible understatement. Governor Reagan and I had a lengthy private conversation about the process of obtaining the signatures. I showed him the letter from the First Presidency and he nodded his head in both approval and admiration for their willingness to call upon the members of the Church to support our efforts. At the conclusion of the meeting he added another vital note, "You have my complete support and endorsement for Proposition 18. I'll be praying for your success."

Near the end of June, now certain that we would be on the November ballot, I was invited to attend a meeting at the prestigious California Club in Los Angeles. The intriguing thing about the invitation was that it came from the people whom I knew to be in the forefront of the opposition to my anti-pornography legislation in the senate and the assembly. I accepted the invitation. When I entered the room there were nine people seated around the table, five of whom were attorneys for the motion picture industry, the slick magazine publishers and distributors, and of all things, one of the major newspapers in southern California. As the meeting went forward, it was obvious that I was alone in more ways than one.

For three hours I responded to the "concerns" raised by the lawyers as to how this legislation that was being submitted to the electorate would stifle freedom of the press or other extensions of First Amendment rights. Never once was an objection to the initiative measure raised that I was not able to overcome by reference to the actual language of the proposed statute and the decisions of the Supreme Court. Just prior to my departure I asked very candidly if they had raised one issue that I had not been able to demonstrate was a needless worry about some First Amendment loss of freedom. No one accepted my challenge, so I asked them pointedly if there was any reason for them to oppose our efforts. No one would give me a direct answer, but I left the room naively thinking that perhaps because of the defense I had been able to make of the language of the initiative they would not choose to oppose us.

Later one of the participants in the meeting told me that before I had reached my car in the basement garage the members of the group had firm pledges in hand for more than three million dollars, all to be used against us. The campaign leading to the November election would be David against Goliath, but David not only had no sling or smooth stones to use in it, but also his right arm would be tied behind his back.

At about this same time I took my family to Utah for a brief vacation. While there I had an appointment with Elder Howard W. Hunter to explain to him our situation. As I was preparing to leave he asked if I would like to receive an apostolic blessing. I assured him that I would be most grateful. He then called on the telephone to Elder Ezra Taft Benson, who agreed to come to Elder Hunter's office to participate in the blessing. The two Apostles then laid their hands upon my head and gave to me a blessing regarding the coming campaign for the enactment of Proposition 18. Among other promises made in their blessing, I was told that I would be given energy and keenness of mind beyond my normal capacities, and that I would be preserved in health and strength throughout the campaign effort on behalf of the ballot proposition. There were several other promises made, one of which was that I would be protected from the forces of evil, and to that end the shield of an apostolic blessing was pronounced upon me.

At the time the newspapers picked up the story that we had qualified for the ballot, the most prestigious public opinion pollster in the state, Melvin Field, conducted a state-wide poll of voters regarding support for Proposition 18. The poll results were seventy-five percent in favor and twenty-five percent against. Now we had to go out into the "trenches" and protect that broad base of public support.

For the next four and one half months (from late June to the election in November) Ernie Schulzke and I were up and down the state on an eighteen- to twenty-hour per day routine of speeches, debates (always the ACLU were only too anxious to debate as long as it was in front of their own supporting audiences), radio talk shows, television interviews, and so forth. Since defending the proposition required a detailed knowledge of the law of obscenity, it was almost impossible to effectively prepare others to accept most of these speaking requests. We prepared a speaker's manual and resource book that enabled others willing to take the time to study it and learn the issues to go out as speakers and advocates in support of the proposition. We ultimately did develop a cadre of people who were quite capable in defending the proposition who could go out to speak to various community groups and organizations.

Still, the burden of the tough confrontations with the media and the debates with the spokesmen for the opposition fell primarily on Ernie Schulzke and myself. It was a grueling task week in and week out. I shall describe just one of these experiences to illustrate what happened.

A television station in San Diego sponsored a one-hour debate on Proposition 18. I would be debating (who else?) the local president of the ACLU in San Diego. One unique aspect of the debate was that the viewing audience would be able to call in and vote for or against the proposition as the debate went forward.

The content of the debate was the same hackneyed nonsense that we had heard so often, the convoluted horror stories of people being arrested, tried, convicted, and sent to jail because they innocently had a photograph of some piece of ancient Greek sculpture showing nude portions of the human anatomy. These individuals knew from the beginning that their assertions were not only patently false but totally contrary to the actual language of the statute itself. Still they persisted, and we showed again and again the absurdity, the falsity of their claims.

During the commercial break midway through the debate, the ACLU lawyer brought out of his briefcase a particularly offensive magazine. As he opened it up the several camera crews on the set crowded around to see the photographs. As he held it up I put my eyes down to concentrate on my notes. One of the women taking phone calls from the listening audience shrieked out, "Hey look, the Senator won't look at the dirty pictures." I unwillingly blushed at the gaze of all on the stage and the place erupted in laughter at my discomfort. Such was the contemptuous attitude of the overwhelming majority of those in the media whom we confronted daily.

It was some slight comfort that the "Yes" vote for Proposition 18 in this debate was more than twice the "No" vote

Not long after Labor Day the overwhelming power of that three-million dollar campaign fund against Proposition 18 began to be felt. On television and in the motion picture theaters appeared advertisements against us starring motion picture actors John Wayne and Clint Eastwood. At that time one of the most popular television programs was about a medical doctor named "Marcus Welby," portrayed by actor Robert Young. He joined Wayne and Eastwood in the advertisements on television against the proposition.

We had the endorsement of Governor Ronald Reagan, and the commitment of entertainer Pat Boone and several other Hollywood personalities who supported our efforts. In order to use their prestige in our behalf we had to be able to create the media and then pay to have it broadcast. All of the funding that we could accomplish raised slightly over fifty thousand dollars. I added another seventy thousand dollars out of my personal political funds. With all of the money we raised (a total of $125,000) we printed and distributed literature in support of the proposition. Again the valiant LDS volunteers were incredibly faithful and vitally important as they undertook the distribution of our literature door to door. When all of the literature we had the money to print had been used, many of these wonderful people used their own funds to pay to have our literature copied so that they could distribute it in their neighborhood. We had no funding for radio, television, or newspaper ads.

But in the end, with the opposition spending more than thirty dollars against us for every dollar we could spend, the result was inevitable. When the vote was counted we lost by the reverse of the ratio of support with which we began in June. The vote tallied on Proposition 18 was seventy-five percent "NO" to twenty-five percent

"YES." One man, the publisher of *Playboy* magazine, had written a check to the opposition for $125,000. His check equaled all of the money that we had been able to raise from every possible source in support of the measure.

The opposition grossly misrepresented the content of Proposition 18. We attempted through the courts to make them cease these lies, but the courts would not grant us any relief. The judge's comment was "there is no enforceable requirement for truth in the political process." The media, the daily newspapers (especially the *Los Angeles Times*) were viciously brutal. The proposition was depicted as the ranting of a group of extremists whose ultimate objective would be to burn books in front of the public library. In many ways it was a wonder that we even got twenty-five percent of the vote.

The massive media campaign against us had a devastating impact on our own supporters. Many of them had never been involved in a political effort before. They had no experience in keeping their composure in the face of intense opposition. As the famous movie stars appeared on television, in the movie theaters, and in newspaper advertisements, all against Proposition 18, the morale of our own supporters was so depressed that many of them ceased their efforts. It was their first taste of battle against this enemy, and in the face of fierce opposition they lost their courage and ran away.

On October 29, 1972, one week before the election, I wrote a letter to Elder Howard W. Hunter, in which I outlined the situation and our inevitable defeat unless some huge miracle could be performed in our behalf. Obviously I was asking for that miracle. Because the letter captures so completely the situation in the atmosphere of the moment, I include some excerpts from it here.

> Dear Elder Hunter,
>
> I write this letter desiring to make you aware of the circumstances in our battle against those seeking to commercially exploit pornography and obscenity in California. This letter is a plea for help in the desperation that comes from one who has nowhere else to go.
>
> During the past week the full force of the opposition's campaign in the mass media has been felt, and it has done much to destroy the morale of our people. Though I had tried to warn them for some time of

what to expect, they really did not appreciate the impact that the radio, television, and motion picture ads would have against us. These ads feature such stars as John Wayne, Robert Young, and others, and the net effect has been to bring a feeling of despair to our supporters, most of whom have never experienced a political campaign before.

Let me briefly recap the campaign for Proposition 18. We based our strategy on the realization that we would not have enough money to do more than print our literature, if that. So we determined that we would rely upon volunteers to carry our literature door to door in a massive grass roots campaign on behalf of the proposition. While we assumed that we would rely greatly upon the Latter-day Saint people to make up the major portion of that grass roots army, we had hoped that others would also join us in the cause. We had counted upon the recruitment of some 30,000 people in order to accomplish our goal of making a contact with every voter residence in the state.

Though I have met with ministerial associations, the leaders of most of the major denominations and principal lay groups of the various churches, our recruitment of people and resources outside of the Church has been minimal. There have been some large cash contributions from non-LDS, but those reflect for the most part my own contact with the sources rather than the merit of our cause.

You are familiar with the process that has been used to mobilize the resources of our own LDS people. The second letter from the First Presidency appeared about the 23rd of August. In it the First Presidency endorsed Proposition 18 and urged the members of the Church (as individual citizens) to assist in the dissemination of facts regarding Proposition 18. At that same time Brother Talmage Jones, a Regional Representative of the Twelve, and I came to Salt Lake and visited with Elder Gordon Hinckley and Brother Marvin Ashton. We specifically discussed with them the manner in which we might interpret the letter of the First Presidency to priesthood leaders in California and also talked of their experience some four years earlier with the "liquor by the drink" issue in Utah.

Upon our return Elder Jones and I began to meet and work with the Priesthood leaders of the stakes in California. As earnestly as we labored, however, it became obvious that little was being accomplished. You were successful in obtaining the approval of the First Presidency for a meeting between you and the California regional representative during the October conference. In that meeting you, along with Elders Benson, Hinckley, and brother Marvin Ashton urged the Regional

Representatives to return to their stake presidents with the strongest possible endorsement of our efforts.

Since that meeting a whole new atmosphere developed among the Church members in California. Our recruitment of both volunteers and financial assistance came to life, and new hope filled our hearts. The months of preparation we had made were now being utilized and our basic campaign strategy seemed like it could be fulfilled. Though the response from Church leaders was far from unanimous or without reservation, the log jam of resistance seemed broken and we were making some meaningful progress.

I had been warning our people, however, that they should be prepared for the massive campaign to be waged against us. Even though they knew it was coming, they did not really understand what it would be until it hit, and the depression and defeatist attitude that have swept through our ranks in the last week has been a near fatal blow to our cause. Our people were able to absorb the opposition of newspapers and of radio and television stations, and they could see the lies and distortions that were being used. But when well-known actors appeared who had the image of "Americana" about them, many of our people panicked. My phone has rung incessantly all week long with messages of defeatism and despair from Church leaders in the state.

Though we are being hurt badly by the massive radio, television, newspaper, and motion picture campaign against us, WE CAN STILL WIN THIS BATTLE IF OUR VOLUNTEERS WILL ONLY GO FORTH AND DO THEIR TASK. If they will but proceed to deliver our literature door to door with a personal message and a plea for our proposition, we will still win.

I am not certain what you can do, but I have an absolute faith that we can prevail if it is important enough to our people to make the necessary sacrifices to win. Only one man on earth has the capacity to awaken them to that dedication, and you are the only one I can turn to with a plea to ask him for that consideration of our plight.

You previously asked me to keep you informed of the progress of the campaign insofar as the activity of the members of the Church was concerned. Though my major purpose in writing this letter is now accomplished I want to share with you some specific aspects of the campaign as it relates to the effort being made by members of the Church.

There are hundreds—perhaps thousands—of instances where wonderful, dedicated people have given hours and hours of time to carry our message and warn their neighbors. They are truly heroes of the war whose reward and identity are known only in heaven. I cannot express how deeply I feel about them—or how much we owe to them for our success thus far. They are the foot soldiers of the royal army of Christ, and they cannot be extolled enough for what they have done.

There are, however, some "weak" spots. Just this Saturday evening I was called at home by a brother from one of the stakes. His opening comment was "My stake president has asked me to coordinate the campaign for Proposition 18 in our stake. What should I do?"

I cannot really express to you my feelings at that moment, realizing that over seven months ago his stake president was told of our needs, and warned that this was not something that could be left until the last minute. Now, with one week remaining before the election, an assignment that should have been made two months ago is given.

The conspiracy by the mass media against us has been vicious. The press have refused to print endorsements of Proposition 18 made by Governor Reagan, the State Chamber of Commerce, the District-Attorney's association, the Los Angeles County Board of Supervisors, the Los Angeles Chamber of Commerce, etc. Our answers to the outright lies and distortions have been ignored. Our state chairman, entertainer Pat Boone, has made a fantastic effort to carry our message to the people. But even he is often unable to penetrate the barrier of censorship the media have raised against us.

We went into the courts to seek some relief because of the complete refusal by the opposition to cease their lies. However, both the trial court and the appellate courts said that we could not be given relief because "truth is not required in a situation like this."

I mention these items to illustrate to you the magnitude of the odds against which we are fighting. The opposition have raised and will spend more than $2 million against us. We have less than $50,000 beyond the money I have loaned to the campaign. You can see why it has been so hard for us to offset the lies and propaganda of the opposition.

The small group of regional representatives working with us have been valiant and unrelenting in their determination to support us. Particularly have Talmage Jones, James Pratt, Daken Broadhead, and John Russon been crucial to our hopes. Each of them in their way have made such a vital contribution that without them we could not have progressed at all. Particularly has Talmage Jones done so much more than we had a right to ask.

One of the most disconcerting problems we have faced has been

the attitude that "these are the last days and we should expect Satan to
triumph now." There have been an amazing number of supposedly
responsible and well-informed Church members who almost seem to
want us to fail on the assumption that things will get worse that much
faster and then "the end will come." I certainly do not read the scriptures to indicate that we are to prepare the earth for the Second Coming
by surrendering to the forces of evil.

As we have previously discussed, another problem has been my
own presence in this effort. Many have suspected that I was trying to
use this issue and the Church for my own political benefit and they have
resented it. In several instances this jealousy has severely weakened
what might otherwise have been accomplished.

Another great problem has been the tendency to procrastinate.
Stake and ward leaders with no experience in the political process have
naively assumed that like "home teaching," this assignment could wait
to the last minute and then be completed. We have pleaded with them to
understand that this is not the case—but to little avail.

Finally we have had some LDS who do not understand the proposition and the law, who have taken a "neutral" position, or even have
opposed us. These people spoke without knowledge, but they were
attorneys or educators and were listened to. That, plus the propaganda
against us, has been successful in frightening off some of our people.

From these observations I would conclude that the priesthood
members need some further instruction before they can become an
effective force for good in the society outside of the Church, and the
instruction and preparation will have to come from you brethren who
can speak with authority.

One other observation may be helpful to you. Under your instruction from President Lee we have done everything possible to keep this
effort from being identified as a "Mormon" undertaking. There is no
question that those instructions were wise and appropriate counsel. The
media have made several efforts to tie our campaign to the Church but
we have avoided this. Having prominent non-LDS people in our campaign hierarchy has been very helpful.

However, we have also lost some strength by virtue of not effectively distinguishing between what the Church stands for in principle
and what the Church as an organization may be attempting to accomplish legislatively. Our local leaders do not seem to have the vision of
the priesthood quorums as a force to be deployed in a righteous cause
absent a direct mandate from the General Authorities. The impression I

have from this experience is that the Lord's counsel in the 58th section to be "actively engaged in a good cause" needs to be clarified for our local leaders insofar as a cause such as this is concerned.

I have been stunned at how little awareness many of our leaders have of the problem of pornography. They never see it, themselves, so they fail to realize how much of it saturates the lives of many of our youth. Particularly do they fail to comprehend how subtle is the process by which sexually arousing movies and books lead our youth into deeper and deeper addiction to this evil. As you know, two stake presidents refused to allow our literature to be circulated in their stakes because it "offended them." Yet every Aaronic Priesthood boy under their responsibility is exposed to such magazines as *Playboy, Penthouse,* and *Esquire,* all of which feature extensive nudity and sexual titillation. We who are mature choose not to see this material—those who are young and unwary become trapped before they know of the danger.

The issue will be determined in this final week. You are familiar with the statement "You can buy anything in this world for money." That will include this election. If our volunteers carry our literature door to door with a personal plea to vote for the proposition, we will have won a tremendous victory over the forces of Satan. The power to win now rests with our local leaders. If they will awaken the saints to a maximum effort of sacrifice we will win. Since California produces about 70 percent of the pornography sold throughout the rest of the country, our success is a matter of national concern.

If there is any way in which you can infuse those who are in local authority to reemphasize the vital nature of our door to door campaign, our telephone efforts, and our newspaper ads with local subscription, it could well make the difference.

In all our travail there is much for which to be grateful and in which to take hope. With my warmest best wishes, I am

> Faithfully yours,
> John L. Harmer

A delightful commentary from one of the "little old ladies in tennis shoes" who worked valiantly in our behalf was contained in the following letter I received. Written by a sixty-nine-year old courageous woman it captures more eloquently than I the reasons for our failure.

Jan. 25, 1973
RE: PROP. 18

Dear Senator Harmer:

In answer to your letter of Nov. 15th—Bishop Harold Southwick passed away in September and Monte Southwick (a relative) is now Bishop of the Willits Ward.

I regret to say that neither the petitions nor especially the brochures generated much enthusiasm up here in the Priesthood. They were all for Prop. 18 I feel sure—but for some one other than themselves to go out door to door. Everyone was too busy.

It's surprising how fast headaches develop when a thing of this sort needs doing. All sorts of ills creep up. I don't mean this to be sarcastic—it's just that it's so discouraging.

If only the Priesthood members would read D&C 98:6–10; 101: 77–78; 134:51, and take it to heart we shouldn't have any problem. The film on pornography was shown several times by Brother and Sister Harris to women's clubs and church groups. The Methodist and Lutheran Church opposed Prop. # 18. Why?

As you know it failed to pass here by about the same percentage as elsewhere—much to the sorrow of those few who worked so hard for it. Because I have carried other petitions, I think this is why this one was dropped in my lap. I did the best I could and had to recruit helpers outside the Church. Members of the J.B.S. chapter pitched in—we covered all the registered voters in the 6 precincts within the city limits and many outside.

I'm sure at least half the people who voted No on 18 thought they were voting for control of obscenity. People don't read—they are glued to TV and that's where Robert Young and Clint Eastwood were. People simply refuse to be responsible for a Constitutional type of Government. I'm not sure but what Harry Hopkins was right. I believe if all the money that was spent on Prop. 18 had been used to buy TV time the results may have been different. It seems impossible to educate the general public except by TV. (With the wrong things.)

At 69 years young I'm ready to go to work on it again if the Spirit would move the Priesthood. Otherwise, I've had it. With plenty of TV coverage and worded so people could vote No it could make it. But voting Yes for something they are against is too much for them. They just don't think. I don't see how it could be worded for a No vote. Do you?

"Sincerely,
(Mrs.) Agnes Carlson"

There is one final post script to the Proposition 18 story. On the last night before the election (Monday) my final campaign appearance on behalf of Proposition 18 was on a television station in Oakland. The program ended at 11:00 P.M. As I drove out of the city toward Sacramento I took one last look back at the temple. Then proceeding toward Sacramento, I realized that something strange was happening to me physically. I literally felt the strength and the vitality that I had come to take for granted during the past four months drain out of my body. Whereas before I could end an eighteen- or twenty-hour day after only four hours of sleep with reserve vitality and energy, I now seriously questioned whether I could make it back to my home in Roseville, just east of Sacramento.

I did arrive home safely, but it was several weeks before I was able to complete even a normal eight-hour day without an intense feeling of exhaustion. The blessing pronounced upon me by Elders Hunter and Benson had been literally fulfilled in many ways. Now I was on my own again, and my body, mind, and spirit took a long time to fully recover.

Proposition 18 was the last real opportunity we had to severely curtail the production and distribution of pornographic material out of California. It is still true today as it was at that time that California produces 75 to 80 percent of all the pornography being distributed throughout the United States in printed or videocassette media. Proposition 18 was defeated in November of 1972. Among the arguments used against it was the false assertion that it would be contrary to current Supreme Court mandates regarding pornography. In the summer of 1973 the United States Supreme Court handed down its decision in *Miller v. California.* The Court in that decision vindicated every defense we had made of the purpose and content of Proposition 18. But without the provisions of Proposition 18 the Court's decision in *Miller* was not nearly as effective as it could have been if Proposition 18 had been voted for by the people of California.

My letter to Elder Hunter correctly identified the elements of defeat. If there is any lesson to be learned of that experience of so many years ago it is that if the membership of the Church is to be mobilized in a similar cause it can only be done with a clear and unequivocal mandate from the leadership of the Church. Whether such a mandate is feasible under the prevailing tax laws without jeopardizing the Church's tax-exempt status is not something I care to comment upon. But, as Whittier wrote, "Of all sad words of tongue or pen, the saddest are these, 'it might have been.' "

Chapter Seven

PORNOGRAPHY
AND HOMOSEXUALITY

Concurrent with the dramatic increase in the volume and the availability of pornography has been the emergence of the conspiracy to make homosexuality and lesbianism accepted as legitimate forms of behavior. Consistent with the pornographer's use of the bizarre and the obscene, the graphic depiction of homosexuality and lesbianism has always been part of the pornographic presentations. Equally consistent with their pattern of working closely in harmony with the pornographers, the motion picture industry has continually moved farther and farther toward open advocacy of homosexuality and lesbianism, and in the legislative and congressional chambers and in the courts the ACLU has aggressively pursued the promotion of privileged status to the practitioners of these deviancies.

There has been a reason for this phenomena that I shall set forth below. First of all, let me recite some of the activities of this well-orchestrated campaign to eliminate the family unit as the fundamental political and social unit of our civilization.

As an illustration of how successful the campaign to make the perversion of homosexuality and lesbianism acceptable has been, I mention a motion picture released in 1968 entitled *Theresa and Isabella* that presumably depicted the homosexual activity of two young girls at a French academy. Although the film exhibited the female breasts and female nudity from the rear, there were no frontal exhibitions of the pubic area in the film. There were scenes of simulated female sodomy and oral sex, but without the now typical closeup of the genitals. By today's MPAA rating standard the film would be given a rating of R at the most, and might even qualify for the PG-13 rating. Interestingly enough, there is no profanity in the film, contrary to the typical use in many of today's PG-13 rated films of many of the profane vulgarities that until recently were heard only in military barracks or back alleys.

Notwithstanding all of that, in 1968 a jury found that the motion picture *Theresa and Isabella* was patently obscene and returned a verdict finding that the film "affronted contemporary community standards" and was "utterly without redeeming social value." In its decision the court noted: "This movie does not attempt to show lesbian homosexuality as a relationship that should be discouraged but rather presents it as a pleasurable sensual relationship that should be encouraged. What social value is there in such a theme? Absolutely none."

We noted in chapter 3 that in 1998 a motion picture containing "profanity, verbal obscenities, strong homosexual innuendos," and in which an open-mouth homosexual kiss between two men is graphically presented, was given a PG-13 rating by the Motion Picture Association of America. Thus in thirty years our society went from a stated position that such a depiction was completely offensive to the moral values of the community, patently obscene, and utterly without redeeming social value, to a point where a film that went significantly beyond the depiction of homosexual conduct in *Theresa and Isabella* is deemed suitable for children thirteen years of age and older. Given that precipitous descent into the abyss of obscenity over the last thirty years, what reason is there to believe that by the end of the next thirty years any restraint will exist to the exhibition anywhere of anything the depraved pornographers can conceive?

In 1980 I became the president of the largest anti-pornography organization in the United States, known as "Citizens For Decency Through Law,"or "CDL" as it was popularly known, with headquarters in Phoenix, Arizona. Interestingly enough, the organization's founders and principal financial supporters were very faithful Roman Catholics, while I, as the president, was an orthodox Latter-day Saint.

CDL gave me the means by which to continue the work against pornography that I had carried on in my elected office and as a practicing attorney. The organization monitored various pornographer's activities, trained prosecutors and law enforcement personnel on how to effectively gather evidence against and prosecute pornographic materials, joined as a "friend of court" plaintiff in many actions against pornographic materials, and distributed newsletters and training materials to citizens throughout the country.

In 1981, in a Phoenix meeting of prosecutors and citizen activists in the battle against pornography, I gave a speech in which I predicted certain developments in the moral climate of the United States. In that speech I specifically identified the then emerging effort to "legitimatize" homosexual conduct as one of the principal goals of the pornography industry. The primary motivating factor for this effort would be the remarkable increase in the active market for pornography, and thus increased profit to the pornographers.

Until the last decade many of the professional psychologists and psychiatrists who have studied homosexual lifestyles commented that homosexuals and lesbians turned to sexual deviancy as an escape from some more deep-seated emotional or psychological problem. Their homosexuality was a means of giving some defensible basis for their immersion in deviancy. They become easy prey to the pornographers, who shamelessly exploit the homosexuals and lesbians and take from them millions of dollars per year. In that 1981 conference I predicted that it would soon become "fashionable" to engage in homosexual and lesbian conduct because of the social pressures to do so aided by the power of the entertainment media to propagandize the acceptability of such behavior.

Within a few years the various predictions I had made came to pass. A well-orchestrated effort to bring homosexuality into the realm of acceptability was carried out through the television, the motion picture, and the slick magazine. A very popular Broadway musical starring Julie Andrews and Robert Preston presented a humorous and very positive image of a homosexual life.

With this type of media support the strategists seeking to make homosexuality acceptable turned to the political arena to claim a privileged status as a distinct but legitimate "special" group. Another arena selected to give dignity and legitimacy to homosexual behavior was the public school classroom. In every arena they were dramatically successful, and in less than ten years homosexuality made the transition from being a shameful form of deviancy to a legitimatized choice of "life-style" which could not be the object of "discrimination" in employment or other associations. The key element of the campaign was to ask the rest of society to consider homosexuals for "what they are," rather than for "what they do."

A classic example of the skill with which this campaign was pursued was to change the nomenclature of this form of sexual deviancy by the use of the word *gay* as describing those of what the press and others euphemistically referred to as "an alternative lifestyle." They were not homosexuals or lesbians, but "gay." As is true with all they do, they took a word that once reflected pure joy and happiness and sullied it with association with sexual deviancy and degenerate values.

The movement to legitimatize homosexuality gained immense financial support from the motion picture industry. Why should Hollywood and the television studios that have grown out of Hollywood fall all over themselves to extol and give dignity to homosexuality? For the same reason why they have always pursued the erosion of morality and virtue: because of the immense profits that were ready to be reaped from this new class of hapless victims. Give legitimacy to the homosexuals and a whole new era opens up offering formerly forbidden themes for the motion picture and television industry. Never mind that millions of lives would be warped and made miserable as a result of this conspiracy. And as ever, silently but gratefully the pornographers could rub their hands in glee as these endeavors gave them greater open access by which to market their own versions of this human deviancy.

In the May/June 1998 issue of the *Leadership Bulletin,* published by the Howard Center for Family, Religion & Society, the following summary of fund-raising on behalf of homosexual and lesbian programs was given. (Reprinted here by permission.)

> In one evening the Los Angeles Gay and Lesbian Center raised $316,000. . . . In support were Hollywood regulars . . . including Kathy

Najimy, Helen Hunt, Woody Harrelson, Cindy Crawford, Kada Pin-
kett, Jennifer Aniston, Ted Danson, and Mary Steenburgen . . . Hon-
orees for the "Women's Night" event March 21: Ellen DeGeneres, California State Assembly Speaker pro tem Sheila Kuehl, and U.S.
Senator Carol Moseley-Braun. . . . Across the country the Gay Men's
Health Crisis raised $450,000 at a February 1 benefit concert featuring
Bette Midler, Lainie Kazan, and Madeline Kahn . . . and Denver-based
software tycoon Till Gill will donate $700,000 throughout 1998 to
homosexual groups in Colorado Springs, Colorado. . . . Why the way?
The Gill Foundation has determined that Colorado Springs has become
a stronghold of the "Christian Right."

What do the homosexual and lesbian organizations do with this
money? Primarily they use it to engage in litigation and legislative
lobbying activities that will entirely eliminate both legal and histor-
ical condemnation of homosexual deviancy. These organizations
have financed the various lawsuits around the country against the
Boy Scouts of America in attempting to overturn the policy of the
BSA against homosexual leaders of Boy Scout troops. Extensive and
highly successful political efforts by the homosexual and lesbian
groups have resulted in the enactment of various state and federal
statutes making it unlawful for employers and other entities to "dis-
criminate" in any way against those who openly espouse the homosexual deviancy.

On October 11, 1987, the media reported that more than two
hundred thousand homosexuals and lesbians participated in a giant
rally in Washington, D.C. The purpose of the rally was to "demand"
that federal legislators grant to them the same rights that were traditionally reserved for heterosexual couples. These included the right
to file joint tax returns, the right to adopt children, the legal recognition of the rights normally associated with a husband or wife of an
employee, and predictably, the special right to be given employment
preferences because they were homosexuals.

In my career as an elected official I had often been involved with
issues generally identified as being concerned with "sex education."
The architects of moral decline in America had long recognized that
if they could effectively use the classroom to propagandize their outlandish philosophy the victory would soon be theirs. So-called "sex

education" classes had the predictable result of increasing the burden of teenage pregnancy and pre-marital sex among high school youth.

Into this situation came the homosexual activists, insisting that young people be taught how to perform homosexual acts as well as heterosexual acts. Illustrated manuals on how to engage in homosexual intercourse soon found their way into the sex education programs of many school districts. Outraged parents were finally awakened to the tragedy and in many instances successfully removed the offensive materials from the classroom. More often than not, however, it remained, and still remains today, as part of sex education curriculum.

In the fall of 1969 the *Los Angeles Times* printed the following report of a meeting in Santa Monica, California, at which I and Dr. Melvin Anchel, M.D., a psychiatrist specializing in counseling of sexually abused children, were the principal speakers.

> State Sen. John Harmer, R-Glendale, Friday night labeled current sex education programs in California schools as the "propagandizing of an outlandish philosophy."
>
> The philosophy—that moral absolutes no longer exist and that all values are relative—is "symptomatic of a broader phenomenon," the senator told a crowd of nearly 500 at John Adams Junior High.
>
> The meeting was sponsored by the Parents Committee for Sound Education founded after the Santa Monica School board began consideration of sex education instruction.
>
> The "phenomenon" is an effort by people who "are trying to undermine the traditions and heritage of the past (sic)," Harmer said. One of the traditions is the sanctity of the family, which is under attack by many sex education courses.
>
> "As the family erodes, our nation becomes weaker," he said, adding that historically, philosophers have regarded the family as the basic political unit.
>
> Harmer said he felt that it was proper and useful for the schools to teach sex as a physiological process, as long as the program is not directed at young children and instructors are well trained.

This and other presentations that I made before similar audiences earned for me the intense hatred of the organizations and

members of the education establishment who promoted the sex education programs that soon became recruiting efforts for homosexuality among youth.

The principal proponent of this type of material for the school
classroom is the SIECUS organization (the Sex Information and
Education Council of the United States). Quoting again from the
Leadership Bulletin May/June 1998, published by the Howard
Center for Family, Religion and Society, here is a summary of some
of the then-current activities of SIECUS.

"(SIECUS) loves 'comprehensive sexuality education' . . .
SIECUS hates abstinence-only education . . . quite naturally
SIECUS has nothing good to say about the next sex education curriculum, *Managing Pressures Before Marriage.* . . . Here are three
guidelines of the new curriculum they have a problem with . . . 1)
'abstinence from sexual activity outside marriage is the expected
standard for all school age children' . . . 2) 'a mutually faithful
monogamous relationship in the context of marriage is the expected
standard of human sexual activity' . . . and 3) 'sexual activity outside
the context of marriage is likely to have harmful psychological and
physical effects' . . . the *SIECUS staff were 'dismayed' by these
guidelines.*"

In a recent review of a book entitled *Saving Childhood* by
Michael and Diane Medved, the author of the review took occasion
to comment on the extensive efforts within the public school sys-
tems to push "sex education" programs that most parents, if aware of
the content, would refuse to allow their children to attend. Then the
reviewer, Yale University Professor David Gelernter, quoted a passage from the book: "Today's education plan to rescue children from
the benighted, old-fashioned, restrictive and prejudicial values that
parents want to impose on them . . . They teach that school is a
source of enlightenment and concern, with its counselors and health
programs and contraceptives freely available. By contrast, home is
dangerous, it's a place where kids can't trust even Daddy's
embrace."

Professor Gelernter then noted: "Educators push for sex and
anti-drug programs—though sex education tends to make children
more sexually active, and anti-drug programs mainly waste time.

Meanwhile math teaching (international comparisons show) has collapsed. Reading-and-writing education is failing (I see the results among Yale undergraduates). History teaching tends to incorporate anti-American lies. And education in civics and morality has reached the point where, as the Medveds write, 'a fear of criticizing anyone else lets students condone the Holocaust. (Who's to say the Nazis were morally wrong?)'"

Finally Professor Gelernter made this observation about the powerful entities behind this demise of dignity in the American schools: "Today's depraved sex education didn't happen by accident; it was invented by people who believe in depravity. And such people have a constituency."

The obvious outgrowth of this strategy is to achieve the legitimization of homosexual and lesbian marriages in the eyes of the law. Then all of the legal rights associated with heterosexual marriage will become available. This particularly concerns the right to adopt children, or to bring the children from a previously heterosexual union into a homosexual one. The ultimate question that society will only ask when it is too late and the consequences have become more obvious is, "What of the children being raised in such circumstances?"

Children introduced into close association with homosexuals are likely to be the victims of two forms of deviancy: the homosexual relationships themselves and the very probable use of the child for pedophelia, or the sexual abuse of children of either sex. The use of the child for the creation of pornographic literature appealing to the pedophile becomes an equally tragic potential. Whatever the ultimate outcome may be of the continuing pressure to give the practicing homosexual or lesbian the legal right to adopt children, the ultimate benefit to the pornography industry will be the many additional potential consumers of the sexually deviant materials.

In case I have not made the point clearly enough, let me state it here in plain, direct simplicity: The overwhelming motivation behind the drive to legitimatize homosexuality and lesbianism is the "profit motive." Hundreds of millions of dollars have come into the hands of the pornographers, the motion picture industry, the ACLU, and the self appointed "spokesmen" for the homosexuals and the lesbians through their advocacy of this perversion. Promoting this destruction of the family unit is an immensely profitable business. In so many pathetic ways, those who should have been at the forefront of opposing this tragic perversion have turned the other way.

PART TWO

THE
SOLUTION

CHAPTER EIGHT

THE LOCAL COMMUNITY

The States have the power to make a morally neutral judgment that public exhibition of obscene material, or commerce in such material, has a tendency to injure the community as a whole, to endanger the public safety, or to jeopardize, in Mr. Chief Justice Warren's words, the States' "right . . . to maintain a decent society."

"In particular, we hold that there are legitimate state interests at stake in stemming the tide of commercialized obscenity, even assuming it is feasible to enforce effective safeguards against exposure to juveniles and to passersby. . . . These include the interest of the public in the quality of life and the total community environment, the tone of commerce in the great city centers, and, possibly, the public safety itself" *(Paris Adult Theatre I v. Slaton* (413 U.S. 49; 1973).

The pornography industry has always been able to immediately grasp the potential financial benefit of an emerging technology. The evolution of the production of pornography from print, to still photograph, to motion picture, to television, to videocassette, to direct satellite broadcast, and now the Internet—all attest to the pornographer's insatiable appetite for increased ability to market degeneracy. Thus it was totally predictable that the pornographers would seek to utilize the rapidly increasing subscriptions to cable TV services as a way to expand their consumer group.

The pornographers always assume that an effort will emerge to stop their invasion of a new medium. This fact of life was simply relegated to the category of the cost of doing business. Because of their vast financial resources the pornographers could be confident that there was always the ability to defeat, or at least significantly delay, the often feeble efforts by law enforcement or motivated individuals to stamp out the new evil. The cable network owners had little or no hesitancy to accept blatantly pornographic material. Their cowardly excuse was to mindlessly assert that "we are not authorized to act as censors or even editors."

Contracts for cable providers were controlled by municipalities. With the emergence of the cable TV industry there also came into being an entirely new arena of economic activity for which the existing laws regarding the broadcast of obscene materials were not adequate. The conflicting claims of jurisdiction also served the pornographer's interests. Was cable transmission a broadcast or not? Was a cable license for an enclosed community an activity of inter-state commerce or only of intrastate commerce? Which prosecutors and which courts had the responsibility to deal with cable, and what laws applied? To the pornographers the answers to these questions were irrelevant, since their defense was always the same. It was only for those who wanted to preserve the moral values of our society that these questions became critical factors in the battle for decency.

In the early 1980s my wife and I brought our family from California to Utah. At that time I was serving as the president of the largest anti-pornography organization in the United States, known as "Citizens for Decency Through Law" (CDL), with headquarters in Phoenix, Arizona. Because of my work at CDL I was aware of the rapidly increasing use of cable to transmit hard-core pornographic materials. Many of the films that we had attacked in the courts as being exhibited in the adult theaters around the country were now showing up on cable TV.

Our work at CDL was to assist local prosecutors in gathering evidence and presenting their case at trial. Whereas the pornography industry had lawyers throughout the country who were experienced and well versed in defending pornography, most prosecutors' offices had little or no prior experience in this arena. Thus it was usually David against Goliath when the issue was in court, except that Goliath won almost nine out of ten times. At CDL our work was to teach David how to beat Goliath.

When a prosecutor called on our organization for assistance we were able to send in one of our several staff attorneys who were former deputy prosecutors and were experienced in prosecuting pornography. That attorney knew the law regarding obscenity, knew the tactics and the attorneys used by the pornographers, and knew how to develop a successful case to prosecute a pornographic item, such as a book or a film.

In December of 1981 CDL sponsored and hosted a meeting in Phoenix of several hundred prosecutors and legislators from throughout the United States At the opening of that conference I made a speech in which I recited where we were at that time in the battle for decency, and what I saw as our options for the future. Following are some comments taken from my remarks to that group:

> I do not believe it is too late—but I believe that it is much later than most Americans realize. I believe that if we do not do something about it now the decline will soon be irreversible.
>
> This year, according to the Gallagher survey of national publications, Americans will spend over four hundred million dollars ($400,000,000.00) in subscriptions to four blatantly pornographic magazines. That four hundred million dollars represents eleven and one-half million subscriptions, and it is reliably assumed that for every subscription there are two and one-half readers. Thus, thirty million Americans, by subscription alone, will, during this year, be influenced by these publications.
>
> These figures relate only to four very commonly known publications, about which the assertion that they are pornographic is constantly eroded by a wider and wider base of acceptance in our society. As the tolerance of our people towards this material increases, the difficulty for the prosecutor and the community to remove the more heinous pornography becomes greater and greater. . . .
>
> The present trend will soon leave us beyond Sodom and Gomorrah. The formerly shameful and hidden perversions of homosexuality and lesbianism are now publicly paraded. Advocates of the unthinkable use of children as appropriate sexual partners are given space and time in supposedly responsible forums. Our arts, our literature, our entertainments have two dominant themes—sex and violence.
>
> As society becomes more desensitized, the frontier of madness moves back. . . . The Federal Bureau of Investigation tells us that the

hard-core pornography industry has now passed the four billion dollar a year mark in revenue, and that figure is increasing rapidly. . . . We truly stand on the brink of an innundation of this material.

By 1995 that figure of four billion dollars had nearly doubled as the videocassette and the Internet opened up vast new ways of marketing filth.

At that time (the early 1980s) many of the communities of Utah were in the midst of granting their first cable licenses, or reviewing existing licenses for renewal. Inasmuch as the CDL had been monitoring the rapidly increasing incidence of pornography on cable, I followed these licensing procedures rather closely. At that time CDL had monitored the broadcast of thirty-four hard-core pornographic motion pictures over cable TV in some part of the country.

When the pornography industry determined to fully exploit the potential market waiting for them in cable television it became necessary to remove the barriers that then existed to the broadcast of obscene and pornographic material over cable. With the American Civil Liberties Union fronting for the pornographers, a lawsuit was initiated in West Pennsylvania (*Midwest Video v. FCC, 571 F2nd 1025, 1979*). The lawsuit resulted in a decision by the United States Supreme Court that effectively removed the authority of the Federal Communications Commission over the program material or content of cable broadcasting.

Following the decision of the Supreme Court in October of 1980, the FCC issued its order FCC 80-608 by which it effectively rescinded its ability to regulate the material content of cable TV broadcasting. From then on the incidence of pornographic material on cable increased dramatically.

Even though the Supreme Court had determined that the federal statutes creating the FCC did not give them regulatory authority over cable, there was still the fact that no cable company could function without a contract from the municipality in which it was located. The obvious thing to do was to include in the contract a prohibition on the broadcast of indecent material. CDL assisted a number of communities in preparing the appropriate language to be included in their license agreement with the cable provider.

This time the most difficult problem we faced in Utah was the lack of concern among the general citizenry, even though the obscene content of cable TV descended lower and lower. In an article published in *TV Guide* on October 30, 1982, there appeared the following article about the *Playboy* channel on cable TV then known as "Escapade." "Every two months Escapade polls 600 subscribers with an eight-page questionnaire. The surveys reveal some surprising information: 42 percent of the viewers are female. . . . But one overriding theme emerges from the raw data: Escapade subscribers want raunchier movies. 'Sure, we get complaints about Escapade,' notes Brian O'Neill, until recently general manager of United Cable TV of Eastern Shore in Ocean City, Maryland. . . . 'About 10 subscribers each month phone up and say that Escapade isn't explicit enough,' says O'Neill. 'Nobody has told me the service is objectionable.' "

Invariably, in my efforts to confront the problem of pornography on cable, the managers of the cable system that carried the program would make that same assertion: "Why are these people so concerned about it?" they would ask. "No one in the community has contacted us with any objections or concerns."

I was dismayed to see that in Utah there was seldom any concern by the licensing community about the issue of including in the license a requirement to ban the broadcast of pornographic material over the cable system. Even when some communities did include in their licensing arrangement with the cable provider a prohibition against the broadcast of "indecent materials" there were no sanctions against the violation of this provision, and any enforcement effort was sporadic at best.

In 1981 the Utah legislature had enacted a statute against the broadcast over cable of "indecent material," which was simply described in the statute as "nudity." The statute was very poorly drafted, and predictably the cable industry soon succeeded in having it voided by the courts.

The next year, 1982, one community in Utah did in fact pass an ordinance prohibiting the broadcast over cable of "indecent material." The ordinance attempted to define what was meant by "indecent material," as being "nudity, which under contemporary community standards is patently offensive." The ordinance did not establish

other criteria that had previously been established by the Supreme
Court in defining what could be proscribed as obscene. It too was
struck down by the courts in litigation filed by the cable industry.

On one occasion when I was present at a licensing hearing before
a city council and had arranged for one of the council members to
pose the question to the license applicant about such a restraint, the
applicant replied that they had no legal authority to "censor" the
materials being broadcast by one of their customers. The answer was
patently false, but what stunned me was that the city attorney agreed
with the response. When it came time for the public to question or
comment I challenged both the applicant's answer and the city
attorney's erroneous concurrence. Then I experienced for the first
time a phenomenon that I was to see repeated many times during the
next year. A member of the city council responded to my comment
by saying, "Well, it isn't our right to deny people their free agency."

I was so stunned by the incredulous nature of the comment that I
simply looked in silent disbelief at the individual who had offered
this inane excuse for avoiding having to confront the forces of evil.
"Could he be serious," I wondered. "Is it conceivable that an elected
official faced with a very clear issue of protecting the moral environment of the community could make such an absurd comment?" I was
to hear that same excuse, usually offered by an elected official, a hundred times before the November election of 1984.

By the way, the member of the city council who had offered a
motion requiring that the license agreement between the community
and the cable service provider include a ban on the broadcast of
pornography with a severe penalty for violating the ban could not
even get another member of the council to second his motion.

At about that time (1982) I was invited to give a speech before
the annual meeting of the Utah Association of Women, an organization that had previously come into existence to defeat the various
ultra-liberal legislative initiatives of the women's liberation movement. In my speech I recited the above history of how the cable
industry had defeated the effort to control the broadcast of indecent
materials over cable in Utah. I then documented some of the hard-
core pornographic materials being broadcast in Utah over cable TV.
The response can only be described as one of "indignant outrage."

The ladies were angry and were ready to go back to the trenches. Over and over the question came from the audience, "Tell us what to do. Tell us how to protect our homes and our community from this material."

While still standing at the rostrum I proposed that they consider sponsoring a statewide initiative measure that would be qualified as both a legislative initiative and a ballot initiative. In essence the initiative measure would be a mandate to the legislature for legislative action. If the legislature failed to act, the initiative measure would be put on the ballot to become an enacted statute by the vote of the people. Because of their own rules involving the procedure to have the organization commit to such a program we decided that I would form a committee to pursue the initiative, and the Utah Association of Women would then be able to endorse the initiative measure and to use their human and financial resources for its enactment.

With the help of the attorneys at CDL we drafted an initiative measure to be put before the voters. Once it was approved by the lt. governor we were able to proceed with printing the petitions (which had to include verbatim the proposed statute) and circulating them throughout the state. A certain percentage of signatures of registered voters had to be obtained in each county. The Utah Association of Women was a true "statewide" organization, and thanks to their effective leadership the petitions were soon being circulated throughout the state. We obtained a total number of signatures representing more than 10 percent of the registered voters who had voted in the last general election.

The measure was drafted by the attorneys at CDL, who had been in every court from the humblest municipal court to the Supreme Court of the United States prosecuting pornography. Essentially the initiative avoided the pitfalls of criminal statutes and instead used a civil remedy available to both the prosecutor and the general public. The essential sanction for violation of the statute's prohibitions was the forfeiture of the cable license.

I think it unnecessary to recite here all of the legal arguments surrounding what became "Initiative A" on the Utah ballot for November 1984. Perhaps a few generalized highlights of the legal principles in support of the initiative will suffice. In reading the following material the reader needs to distinguish between "political" issues and "legal" issues. Much of the confusion and the very sad results surrounding the Utah efforts to control the broadcast of obscene materials on cable were the result of political considerations that were allowed to obscure or diminish the legal issues that had to be resolved. If the political leadership in the state had been willing to support Attorney General David Wilkinson's efforts the results may well have been entirely different, and the moral climate of the state of Utah would be much better.

The fundamental legal issue involved with Initiative A was whether cable programming amounted to "broadcasting" in the same manner as network broadcast television. The significance of that issue was that, through both judicial decree and the regulatory pronouncements of the Federal Communications Commission, the standard of "decency" that was required of regularly broadcast radio and television was well established. The essential thrust of Initiative A was that cable would be required to abide by the same standard of decency as that of broadcast radio and television.

There was also the issue of whether the current state statutes regarding the sale and distribution of pornographic material could be used to prosecute the production and distribution of pornography over cable television. The federal statutes involving "broadcast" of obscene materials might or might not apply to cable. The issue was then whether the local statutes involving the "exhibition" of obscene materials could apply to a television screen receiving a signal transmitted over a cable network.

An issue that was both legal and one of public policy was the matter of protecting children from the pervasive amount of pornography that was now coming into the home through cable. One of the worst mistakes made by the courts in dealing with pornography was to separate the legal status of pornography made available to children from that available to adults. In a well-intentioned but disastrously misguided effort to protect children from the harm of pornography, the courts, the congress, and state legislatures had imposed penalties for the sale and distribution of pornography material to children. Once the courts, state legislatures, and the Congress separated children from adults for special consideration with regard to the production and distribution of pornography there was an immediate legalization of the same pornographic materials for adults. Much of the debate surrounding the cable decency act had to do with the suitability of material for children, the "right" of parents to allow children to view whatever came into the home, and the need of society to protect children whose parents did not or could not supervise their viewing of cable materials.

The legal issues of the responsibility of the cable system operators as opposed to the specific customer who actually used the cable operator's system to broadcast the obscene material, and the evidentiary requirements to prosecute violators of the statute were also hotly debated. Obviously, if the same standard applicable to the owners and operators of radio and television stations were applied to cable, then the cable industry had a well-defined set of criteria for dealing with both of these issues. The operator's assertion that the decency in cable statute would put them in a position of being exposed to criminal liability for violating a standard too vague to be understood was classical media double-talk.

In an article that appeared in the October 16, 1982 issue of the *Deseret News,* authored by staff writer John Robinson, the following summation of the situation in Utah was given.

> The approach of the citizen groups and some city governments is basically this: Ban the offensive matter. If no one can see it no one can be harmed by it. They feel the same restraints should be placed on the fast-growing cable TV industry as are practiced with commercial television.
>
> That solution elicits a strong cry of "foul" from the cable TV promoters, who charge infringement of rights. Their solution is this: If you don't like what's being offered on the movie channels then don't subscribe to them. Stick to the basic cable TV package that includes sports and news stations and some others such as WGN out of Chicago. . . . If you do like the movie channels, subscribe to them and be responsible for prohibiting your children from seeing what you don't want them to see. But whatever you decide, don't try to dictate what your neighbors can see in the privacy of their homes.

There is a classic summary of the skillful rhetoric of the cable system owners and managers. Be "responsible" they would say, which is to say, do not expect us to be "responsible," it is bad for profits. "Make certain your children do not watch programming you consider offensive . . . but don't try to dictate to your neighbor what they can see in the privacy of their homes."

The duplicity and the shallowness of these arguments were never an impediment to their being offered. As noted in that same article, the ACLU was in the forefront of the legal and public debate over the broadcast of pornography on cable TV. They had to earn the money that was so bounteously provided to them by the motion picture and the television industries.

In that same article my own efforts were summarized as follows:

> Harmer, an attorney and former state senator and lieutenant governor of California, is a veteran of the anti-pornography movement. [He] is a former president of the Phoenix-based Citizens for Decency Through Law and spearheaded successful efforts to get an anti-pornography measure on the California ballot in 1972.
>
> Harmer, at the urging of representatives from various citizen groups, has written a statewide initiative to ban indecent material from cable television. . . . He said backers must gather 32,000 signatures to place the measure before the Legislature in January. He hopes to obtain 62,000 valid signatures by the December deadline because that number would qualify the initiative for the ballot in case the Legislature doesn't pass it, he said. . . .
>
> Harmer estimates that 30 percent of the R-rated films now being offered to Utah cable subscribers would not meet the decency standards of the initiative without being edited.

After the appropriate signatures had been gathered the legislative leadership met with the author to propose a "compromise" that would enable the legislature to act on the matter without having to adopt the exact language of the initiative measure as endorsed by the signatures of 10 percent of the state's registered voters. In an effort to cooperate with the legislature the author agreed to forgo any further demand that the legislature enact the precise language as prepared by the attorneys at CDL as long as the legislative statute would accomplish the same objective. When it became obvious that the legislature's effort was going in the wrong direction the author proceeded to facilitate the inclusion of the initiative measure on the 1984 November election ballot, where it appeared as "Initiative Measure A."

In the events that unfolded the legislature foolishly opted to add the "late night exception" to the prohibitions in the statute that was contained in Initiative A. The author warned the legislators repeatedly that what they were doing was inviting the cable industry to use the late night exception (11:00 P.M. to 7:00 A M.) for the broadcast of more pornographic material. As usual, the legislators were far too easily influenced by the representatives of the broadcast industry. The legislators were told and generally believed to be true the assertion that the initiative statute was "patently unconstitutional" (it most clearly was not) and that the proponents of the decency in cable legislation were primarily overzealous housewives who were being manipulated by the author for his own political ambitions.

The result was that the legislature, by accepting the amendments proposed by the cable industry, actually legalized the broadcast of pornographic materials from midnight to dawn. They also opened the door for legal challenges to the statute that could have been avoided if the original "Cable Decency Act" as contained in the initiative measure had been left alone.

The issue of contractual freedom was continually raised by the cable industry. They contended that the contracts into which they had entered, such as the one with HBO, obliged them to act as a "pass through" for the material being presented without presuming to exercise editorial or censorship control over the content. However, our repeated requests to obtain copies of said contracts were continually refused by all of the parties involved.

The industry actually had the temerity to assert that the films being broadcast over cable were "family-type" movies that had been exhibited in neighborhood movie theaters. Why or how they thought that such an outrageous misstatement of fact would go unchallenged remains one of many mysteries surrounding this issue. The fact is that we had recorded the broadcast of a number of hard-core X-rated pornographic motion pictures that had been broadcast over cable in Utah. Some of these films had been successfully prosecuted in other states as hard-core pornography and were still being broadcast over cable TV in Utah.

In the 1983 session the legislature passed Senate Bill 309 (S.B. 309) as the "Decency In Cable TV Act." The attorney general, David Wilkinson, advised the governor in writing that in his opinion the act was "constitutional" and that the legislative history of the act confirmed that its intent and content were adequate to protect any innocent party from mistaken prosecution. Notwithstanding all of the above, S.B. 309 was then vetoed by the governor. The governor's veto message was written by the cable industry. The veto message egregiously misrepresented the content and the effect of the bill.

The author then went to the state capitol and began a series of meetings with legislative leaders regarding an override of the governor's veto. On April 20, 1983, the author showed the legislators some examples of indecent programming recently recorded from cable broadcasts in the state of Utah. Many of the scenes included full male and female frontal nudity. The sexual intercourse scenes did not show a close-up of the human genitals in penetration, but repeatedly exhibited male and female simulated sexual intercourse. There were many scenes of sadomasochistic torture of females associated with various forms of sexual perversion.

A number of legislators from both houses declined to meet with us or to view the video presentation. Those with whom I spoke personally simply said that it was not a problem with which they desired to become "involved." Others were offended that we would even ask them to view such "horrible things." The fact that these "horrible things" were being carried into the living rooms of homes all over the state and that our entire endeavor was to eliminate this evil never seemed to be understood.

One of the legislators actually said to me, "I'm neutral on this issue. I don't care whether it succeeds or not. My constituents are more worried about other things."

That phrase, "I am neutral on this issue," haunted me for several weeks. Finally I decided to write a monograph that would set out the critical policy issues involved with the phenomenal spread of pornography throughout the country. The result was the writing and publication of a fifty-two page monograph entitled, *"To My Neutral*

Friends.'' In the hope that it would make a difference I paid for the printing and distribution of five thousand copies to elected officials and community leaders throughout the state.

Both houses of the legislature voted resoundingly to override the governor's veto of S.B. 309. That guaranteed that the matter would now be in the federal courts for several months.

The various individuals who had been responsible for the drafting and circulation of the initiative petitions then met to decide whether or not to go forward with placing the statute on the ballot for the November 1984 general election. The legislature's enactment (S.B. 309) had not been the one contained in the circulated petitions.

In a brief before the court on the issue of the constitutionality of the legislature's bill (S.B. 309) the attorney general noted: "that the act (S.B. 309) was intended to leave some (broadcast) time open for distribution of indecent material, rather than prohibit it 24 hours a day."

This clumsy effort by the legislature to "buy off" the opposition of the cable industry by giving them an eight-hour window in which to broadcast indecent materials was pathetically inadequate. What it did accomplish was to persuade the individuals and organizations in support of the Decency in Cable initiative to go ahead with placing the measure on the ballot for the November 1984 election. Thus it was designated by the office of the lt. governor as "Initiative A."

During the next four months the author appeared before civic groups and service clubs, on radio and TV talk shows, defending and explaining the content of Initiative A. There were the usual debates with the attorneys for the ACLU. In the beginning the public opinion polls showed an overwhelming base of support for the measure. However, as had happened twelve years earlier in California with Proposition 18, the power of the industry with its money and the amazingly naive assertion by many local ecclesiastical leaders within the Mormon community that the initiative measure was denying people's "free agency" defeated the proposal at the polls.

Apparently *"To My Neutral Friends"* had either never been read or, if read, had failed to make a persuasive case for our cause. For every person in the state who voted for the initiative measure two voted against it.

After the votes were counted and the measure had failed to pass, a newspaper article appeared in which the chairman of HBO took total credit for the defeat of the measure. In the *Deseret News* of Monday, June 3, 1985, was an article captioned, *"HBO Financed the Utah Opposition to 'Initiative A,' "* and there appeared under the byline of Joseph Walker, television critic, the following in the article filed from Phoenix, Arizona:

> And you thought it was Utahns who defeated the cable TV censor-ship initiative in last November's election.
>
> Not so, according to HBO Inc. chairman and chief executive officer Michael Fuchs.
>
> Speaking to about 70 of the nation's television editors at the National Cable Forum here [Phoenix] last Friday, Fuchs said HBO led the fight against 1984's legislative Initiative A. "We have been fighting censorship battles all over the nation," Fuchs told the editors. "On the night of the Reagan landslide the most conservative state in the nation (Utah) defeated a cable TV initiative by a two-thirds majority. I hope that sent a message to the rest of the country."
>
> Asked about the extent of HBO's involvement in the controversial Utah election, Fuchs said: *"We ran it"* (emphasis added). Later he added that his company worked closely with TCI, a Salt Lake City-based communications company.
> "We financed the opposition to the initiative," he said. "We solicited help from other cable companies, but they didn't give much because they knew HBO was taking care of it."
>
> So how much of HBO's cash did it take to keep Utah safe for cable TV?
>
> "I'm not sure," Fuchs said. "It wasn't a gigantic amount. But we felt responsible for doing what we had to do to keep HBO in Utah."
>
> You mean if the initiative had passed HBO might have pulled out of the state, even though the law would have applied only to a limited number of programs?
>
> Fuchs shrugged his shoulders. "I don't see how we could have stayed," he said, "We're not in the habit of allowing our shows to be censored."

In that same month of June 1985, HBO broadcast into Utah a film done exclusively for HBO and not intended for theatrical distribution in which a simulated sexual intercourse scene was graphically presented, and then, a few minutes later, the male in the sex scene had his throat cut by another sexual partner of the female. Leaving nothing to the imagination, his blood was shown spattering all over the windshield of his car. This is the type of intellectual freedom that HBO's battle against "censorship" was protecting. This is the content of protecting other people's "free agency" as was so mindlessly asserted by local "active" LDS community leaders throughout the state.

It was that constant hiding behind the misapplication of the doctrine of agency that was so stunning to me. Time and time again I encountered throughout this process this assertion, in a manner of myopic self-righteousness, of the right that others had to exercise their "free agency." No matter the fact that the exercise of that agency would critically pollute the moral climate of the community and corrupt the youth. The parents of Kelly Hulme and the families of the victims of Ted Bundy and Gary Bishop might have a response to make concerning this shallow use of a righteous principle as an excuse not to confront the powers of evil.

The other lesson from Initiative A that was burned into my consciousness was the ease with which presumably committed LDS leaders and members were able to be manipulated by HBO and others. We repeatedly had LDS lawyers who had never once spent a day in court on a First Amendment issue telling us that the initiative was "patently" unconstitutional. When the authors of these statements could be confronted, without exception they admitted that they had never read the initiative petition but were quoting materials supplied to them by others. Guess who!

Not to be outdone, the Utah League of Women Voters actually printed and circulated to the voters a "non-partisan" summary of the November 1984 ballot in which they stated that "if Initiative A is passed a person could be prosecuted under the law for allowing indecent material to be received in their own home on their own television screen." Since this outrageously false and absurd statement was printed and distributed within the week before the election there was nothing that we could do to stop it. By the time we could have gone to court and proved its falsity the election would have been long past.

It was my experience in other states where I was involved with anti-pornography efforts that the League of Women Voters would consistently oppose every attempt to fight pornography and never seemed to have any qualms about totally misrepresenting the truth with regard to the problem and efforts to combat it.

Throughout the campaign for Initiative A, whenever the "free agency" issue was raised, I would quote in response the following statement from President N. Eldon Tanner, of the First Presidency.

> People who argue that they have their constitutional rights and want to use what they call their free agency to accomplish unrighteous ends abuse the idea of free agency and deprive others of their constitutional rights. While many of our problems are caused by those who are deliberately trying to further their own selfish and devilish interests, there is also a vocal, misled minority which is responsible for other problems as they exist in our country and in our communities.
>
> It is also time we realized that these are all Satan's ways of destroying mankind. Now, what must we do?
>
> If there is pornography or obscenity in bookstores, on television or radio, or in places of entertainment, if there are those who would make more easily available to the young and inexperienced alcohol and its attendant evils . . . and if we are threatened with the passage of laws which violate the commandments of God, it is our duty and responsibility as individuals to speak out, to organize, and to protect ourselves and our community against such encroachments.
>
> It is far more important that we react effectively against the immorality and evil in our communities which threaten the morals and the very lives of our children. (*Seek Ye First the Kingdom of God* [Salt Lake City: Deseret Book, 1973], pp. 88–89)

Several weeks after the 1984 November election I received a telephone call from President Tanner. The only other time I had ever spoken to him was while I still lived in California. I had no idea that he knew who I was or where to find me. It was a short conversation, but directly to the point. He thanked me for making the effort with Initiative A, he counseled me not to be discouraged, and then he said: "Most people who try to accomplish something important in righteousness suffer more defeats than victories. The critical thing is to never give up, to keep trying to do anything you can in the fight against evil." I never spoke to him again, but his kindness and encouragement have been one of the most prized memories of my life.

The final battle in the voting booth over Initiative A was not decided on the issue of the facts, the truth, or concern for the long range future of our society. It was decided solely on the basis of who had the most money to spend influencing the public opinion. By and large the public had little or no desire to inquire into the substance of the issues involved. I traveled up and down the state to attend and speak at public forums on the issue. Almost invariably the local sponsor of the event would apologize to me for the small number of people present. "We did our best to publicize it and get people to come," he or she would say. Then would come the summation that would be repeated consistently up and down the state: "There just doesn't seem to be any real interest."

The demand for more and more explicitly obscene material was filled by the "pay per view" cable channels and the satellite TV channels to which individuals could subscribe by purchasing their own home satellite TV antennae. But the regular cable TV channels continued to move more and more into the realm of sexually explicit materials. The erosion of public concern about the sordid nature of the content of these programs has allowed the networks and the cable TV producers to bring ever more obscene materials into the home.

I conclude this chapter by quoting again from the Supreme Court's decision in *Paris Adult Theater I v. Slaton,* in which the court commented on the validity of the efforts by society to deal with the issues involved in the cable TV debate:

> It concerns the tone of the society, the mode, or to use terms that have perhaps greater currency, the style and quality of life, now and in the future. A man may be entitled to read an obscene book in his room, or expose himself indecently there. . . . But if he demands a right to obtain the books and pictures he wants in the market, and to foregather in public places—discreet, if you will, but accessible to all—with others who share his tastes, then to grant him his right is to affect the world about the rest of us, and to impinge on other privacies. Even supposing that each of us can, if he wishes, effectively avert the eye and

stop the ear (which, in truth, we cannot), what is commonly read and seen and heard and done intrudes upon us all, want it or not.

Understandably those who entertain an absolutist view of the First Amendment find it uncomfortable to explain why rights of association, speech, and press should be severely restrained in the marketplace of goods and money, but not in the marketplace of pornography." (*Paris Adult Theatre I v. Slaton,* 413 U.S. 49; 1973)

CHAPTER NINE

THE OPENING OF
THE FLOODGATES

Just as they did with prior technological advances, the pornographers were quick to grasp the incredible opportunities to reap immense profits from pornography on the Internet. Even they were not prepared, however, for the inundation of competition that the Internet made possible. It is now reliably estimated that there are more than one hundred thousand different sites for pornography on the Internet, and the number increases by three to four hundred a day. There is now available on the Internet everything from the most sophisticated and technologically modern reproduction of pornography (including, of all things, "interactive" pornography) to the most amateurish and crude presentations imaginable.

But the Internet brought to light another even more frightening phenomenon—pornography from those whose only motive was the creating and sharing of obscenity for the sake of its degenerate representations with no financial cost to the consumer. What the overwhelming volume of pornography on the Internet has taught us is that the addiction to this evil is a worldwide perversion.

The other aspect of pornography on the Internet that should strike fear into the heart of all decent people has been the use of the Internet by pedophiles (those who prey on children for sexual gratification) to entice children and young teenagers into their clutches through the use of Internet "chatrooms."

The "chatroom" is one of the diverse uses of the Internet that many parents do not even realize exists. In the "chatroom" individuals talk to each other in real time (instantaneously) over the Internet. The "chatroom" is the target of choice for the pedophile, who is constantly looking for the opportunity to persuade a young user of the "chatroom" to agree to a secret meeting.

On February 10, 1998, the United States Senate Commerce Subcommittee with jurisdiction over communications received the following testimony from Detective Daryk Rowland, of the Huntington Beach, California Police Department.

My name is Daryk Rowland. I am a detective with the Huntington Beach, California Police Department and a member of the Southern California Regional S.A.F.E. Team. One of my assignments is to monitor and investigate criminal activity occurring on the Internet, especially those crimes dealing with child pornography and child sexual exploitation. I have participated in numerous cases which resulted in the arrest and conviction of child molesters who contacted their child victims on the Internet and on-line services.

My purpose today is to communicate to you the immense danger that exists for children from sexual predators and hard-core adult and child pornography available on the Internet to children by their use of personal and school computers.

Because of unfiltered or unsupervised access to the Internet and on-line services, children are being enticed and lured away from home, sexually molested, and victimized through the distribution of child pornography.

With a simple floppy disk inserted into a school computer, a child can run a program that will allow him to access the Internet Relay Chat. From there, the student has access to thousands of pornographic images and the ability to have conversations with strangers that would otherwise not likely occur. Students can access free, personal, anonymous e-mail accounts from school and converse instantly with strangers they meet on the Internet. There are also several programs available that can tell a child when someone he has met on the Internet is online and available to chat. All of these programs can operate on a computer at home or school.

Sexual predators who want to molest children have learned very fast how to communicate with and lure children. They are feeling much safer in their own homes to contact children by computer. They no longer have to wait at the shopping mall or near a park or school and they can do it at anytime of the day or night. All they need is Internet access or an on-line service to begin to contact children.

" . . . Many Web sites contain sexual and violent images that are free for children to view. These images include everything from soft-core porn, frontal nudity, bestiality, defecation, urination, and hard-core torture and "snuff" images.

Detective Rowland's testimony was an incredible litany of specific examples of how children and young teenagers were lured into sexual molestation by being allowed to engage in unsupervised "chatroom" activity on the family computer over the Internet. He then went on to point out that far too often the users of computers on the Internet in schools have no supervision whatsoever, or very passive irresponsible supervision. All of this, he asserted, leads to high possibility for tragedy in the lives of thousands of young people.

A vivid insight into the magnitude of the use of pornography over the Internet is found in the following wire service story written by Catherine Dressler and filed by Associated Press on Wednesday, June 28, 1995.

PITTSBURGH (AP)—Cyberspace has taken the embarrassment out of obtaining pornography in all its manifestations—from bestiality to pedophilia to sadomasochism—and consumers are taking advantage, a study shows.

Carnegie Mellon University's Martin Rimm led a team of more than two dozen researchers in the most comprehensive study to date of online pornography. For 18 months, they surveyed 917,410 sexually explicit images, stories and video clips available by computer and studied computer records of online activity. . . .

The study found pornography is one of the largest, if not the largest recreational uses of computer networks. . . . Half the 8.5 million images called up in the last five years from commercial adult bulletin boards nationwide depicted pedophilia, bestiality, bondage, sadomasochism, transsexualism, and sex involving urination or defecation.

"Until recently, these types of images have often been hard to obtain, even in many adult bookstores," Rimm said. "The World Wide Web is making access to many of these images as easy as a few clicks of a button."

In a typical week, 83.5 percent of the digitized photos transmitted over Usenet news groups were pornographic, the researchers found.

Not all of these sources cost money, although the more power-fully graphic and professionally prepared ones are only available by purchase. Many, however, are simply created and exhibited by neurotic individuals who delight in the presentation and distribution of the vulgar, the vile, the degenerate, the truly obscene.

The Internet's explosive growth gave a world-wide opportunity for the mentally and morally depraved to exchange pornographic images of every description. Particularly avaricious in their conduct were the pedophiles. Of the estimated one hundred thousand pornography sites on the Internet, a huge number are those associated with child pornography.

The ever-present tragedies of pornography have begun to appear more and more frequently in association with the Internet. The most pathetic of these is the use of the Internet by the pedophiles who prey on young children and in a number of documented instances are managing to arrange to secretly meet and seduce young children by virtue of initially contacting them over the Internet. The entire issue of protecting children from this type of tragedy while enabling them to take advantage of the marvelous benefits of the Internet is now one of the most critical challenges facing today's parents of young children.

On Wednesday, September 2, 1998, a worldwide effort was made by law enforcement officers from fourteen countries to make an effective impact on the volume of this material being circulated over the Internet. The following account of that effort comes from the *Washington Post:*

> Law enforcement agents in the United States and 13 other countries yesterday raided nearly 200 suspected members of an Internet child pornography ring, a secretive network described by authorities as the largest and most prolific ever uncovered.
> The U.S. Customs Service, which seized computers from 32 American suspects yesterday in 22 states, said the on-line "Wonderland Club" required all members to possess thousands of sexually explicit images of children, some of them as young as 18 months. Club members then used secret passwords to meet in private Internet hideaways, where they traded the images "like baseball cards," officials said. The ring was targeted for possessing and distributing child pornography, but

in some cases the images pictured club members molesting their own relatives, the officials said.

Officials around the world described the Wonderland raids as the most extensive child porn sting in history and as a troubling glimpse of the future of law enforcement. The digital age, they said, has made it much easier to commit crimes like child pornography, money-laundering and intellectual property theft, while erasing traditional borders between nations. . . .

The Wonderland investigation also illustrated the wide reach of cyberporn throughout this country, in tiny towns and big cities, among the lowly and the elite. Search warrants were executed in communities from Brooklyn to Conroe, Texas, and the American suspects included a scientist, a law student, a medical student and a schoolteacher.

. . . They created a private chatroom accessible only to members, who were only given its password after receiving an introduction from another member and demonstrating their access to pornographic material. (Michael Grunwald, "Global Internet Porn Ring Uncovered," *Washington Post*, September 3, 1998, p. A12)

As if the entire situation were not depressing enough, a federal judge recently ruled that when these pedophiles do end up in prison where they belong they will have a "constitutional right" to keep their sexually explicit materials with them in their cells. The following is from an article in the *Wall Street Journal* of July 22, 1998, written by Dennis Saffran, a regional director of the Center for Community Interest.

Pinups for Pedophiles, the Latest Legal Right

In 1994, spurred by the murder of seven-year-old Megan Kanka, members of a New Jersey task force on child molestation toured the state's Avenel correctional facility for "repetitive and compulsive" sex offenders. It was Avenel that had treated Jesse Timmendequas, the man who killed Megan. The task force members were stunned to find nude pinups and soft-core porn magazines in many cells. Lawmakers on the task force recommended that Avenel ban such sexually explicit material; the Legislature and Gov. Christine Todd Whitman enacted the ban earlier this year.

But last month a federal judge enjoined enforcement of the law, ruling in favor of two pedophiles who argued the porn ban violates their

First Amendment rights. . . . The judge's ruling and the Attorney General's acquiescence to it, present a case study in legal excess: the tendency among many in the legal profession to carry reasonable liberal doctrines to the point of absurdity. . . .

A final irony: In some sexual-harassment cases, the presence of soft-core porn in the workplace has been found to create a "hostile work environment." Thus, a prison clerk who hangs a Playboy pinup in his cubicle could be liable for damages, but under Judge Wolin's ruling a convicted serial rapist has a fundamental right to hang one in his cell.

One of the problems for parents is the fact that a child using the Internet can innocently stumble upon a hard-core pornography site without ever intending to do so. A student attempting to obtain information for a school essay assignment can enter a word into the search engine for the Internet Service Provider (ISP) and find among the many responses half a dozen hard-core pornography sites that are listed right with the legitimate responses. Usually the pornographers include photographs of what is further available by just clicking the mouse on that site.

The United States Congress reacted to the vile nature of what was appearing on the Internet with the enactment in 1996 of the "Communications Decency Act" (CDA). During the hearings on the CDA testimony was given to demonstrate the incredible growth of hard-core pornography on the Internet and the ease with which children can obtain access to this material. In addition, there were repeated demonstrations of how someone quite innocently would find themselves in the middle of hard-core pornography because they had sought out some subject that would seemingly have no relationship to pornography.

As an example, a high school student doing research on the book *Little Women* could enter a search request under that subject and could end up with the graphic depiction on the screen of hard-core child pornography that had a Web site name similar to "Little Women." The Congress received testimony giving multiple examples of similar situations.

Upon the passage of the CDA the pornography industry's affiliated entities—the motion picture producers, the television industry, and their bought and paid-for lackeys, the ACLU—immediately filed the predictable litigation claiming the CDA to be an infringement of "free speech" under the first amendment. Their litigation was ultimately successful.

The Internet has become so satiated with pornography that it is well within the bounds of accuracy to say that with the Internet there is now no barrier to the distribution of hard-core pornography directly into the home. What's more, the most extensive research and development on how to use the Internet for "interactive" sexual experiences is being carried out by the producers of hard-core pornography. Their objective is to enable the recipient to vicariously experience every form of sexual conduct in a manner so close to reality that many would prefer that experience to "the real thing." Preliminary testing of their new technology suggests that they have come very close to achieving that goal. When that happens, we will truly have entered an era of human history that makes all previous accounts of all-pervasive moral iniquity pale into insignificance.

As always, there is the profit motive. The more graphic, the more powerful the vicarious experience, the more addictive it becomes. Just as heroin far exceeds ordinary tobacco in its ability to produce euphoria and dependancy, so the truly serious pornographers are working intensely to perfect a product that will capture an individual far more compellingly and with far greater self-destructive power than even heroin or cocaine. That is what they are determined to achieve with "interactive" pornography on the Internet.

In an article in the March 1995 issue of *Glamour* magazine, Margaret Wertheim, a science writer, describes the advances in the technology for what is referred to as "virtual reality" as portrayed on the computer monitor screen. She recites the significant technological advances of the last several years in achieving "virtual reality" through interactive computer programs. She then poses the following questions:

> Can it be long before more sinister cyberporn fantasies are available? What is to stop anyone from making games in which virtual women are hurt, tortured or even killed as part of the erotic thrill? After all, they would only be collections of bits and bytes.
>
> The prospect of such scenarios highlights a danger of the rapidly increasing realism of computer simulations. . . . Once tactile feedback

devices are added, that blurring will become even greater. A not-incon-
siderable concern with this technology is that it will be used to give
people ever more realistic, simulated experiences of violent and
degrading fantasies.

    . . . I suggest that the possibility of such "harmless fun" is some-
thing we should be concerned about. Just as violence in television
drama inures us to real violence, virtual reality has immense potential
to inure us to violence and sexual degradation. In immersion virtual
reality, your brain experiences the fantasy as reality. . . . With virtual
reality, logic takes a backseat to sensual perception. My guess is that it
would be a shorter step from violent magazine porn to actual violence—particularly for a viewer who might already be a little off-kilter.

    Even apart from the psycho factor, can we really look with equa-
nimity upon the possibility of a future in which any and all fantasies
might be available at the touch of a keyboard? How would you feel, for
instance, if you discovered that a male friend or partner engaged in violent sexual acts with a virtual woman? For those who doubt the need for
concern here, imagine instead that the friend was engaging in sex with
a virtual child. It is no more difficult to visually render a young girl (or
for that matter, a young boy) than a grown woman—and in none of
these cases would anyone *really* be hurt.

Thus we are faced with the fact that we shall enter the twenty-
first century having perfected the ability of anyone to vicariously
experience in the privacy of his or her own home any and every
deviancy that the perverted minds of the pornographers can create.
The technology will exist to enable the participant to experience
every sensation that could come with the "real" experience. Notwithstanding the fact that thousands of years of experience in how people
learn have proven conclusively that this is the most powerful form of
learning (that is, vicariously experiencing the reality) the pornographers and their minions in the ACLU, in academia, and the extreme
left still continue to insist that there is no evidence of any relationship
between viewing or experiencing pornography and actual behavior or
conduct.

    Would these same academicians be willing to concede that there
is no relationship between what happens in their classrooms and the
knowledge gained by a student? Never!

As was true with the cable providers, so the Internet Service Provider (ISP) refuses to attempt to exercise any control over the content of Web sites sold to customers or the use of the interactive sites such as "chatrooms" by the degenerate pedophiles. As was also true with the cable subscriber, the ISPs argue that a subscriber is a "consenting adult," and that society has no valid right to pry into the choices made by such adults. The fact that all hours of the day and night find children and youth under the age of "consent" surfing the Internet is a reality that the providers dismiss as being irrelevant. "Somewhere that child or youth has a responsible adult who can make certain that any undesirable materials are filtered out before receipt into that home," they assert. To give any credence at all to the claims by the providers that they cannot be concerned about things that may never happen is to assume that none of them have ever had children.

Of particular concern to all parents is the fact that computers in public schools and libraries that subscribe to an Internet service give complete access to all of the filth imaginable. Repeatedly librarians and schoolteachers have argued that it would be a violation of their commitment to "academic freedom" to expect them to interfere with a child who is using the computer in their office or library to access pornography. Absent the intense efforts of a community of determined parents, children and youth of all ages can access the most lurid and indecent of materials over the Internet even if every precaution has been exercised in the home to prevent them from doing it there.

Homosexual and lesbian alliances have formed through the Internet, and shamelessly they use it to proselyte new participants in their deviancy. The also have been in the vanguard of efforts to oppose any type of regulation of the Internet. They, along with the ACLU, have been the first to appear at legislative hearings to oppose efforts to address the critical need to bring the abuses of the Internet under control.

Typically absent from any meaningful effort to assist in bringing the use of the Internet under some regulatory control that will make it possible to suppress this type of activity are the feminists. While a few have come forward to speak in defense of truth and virtue in this situation, most feminists are basically anti-family and hate white male patriarchy. To them, the Internet is just one more means of achieving their own agenda of a social structure in which the family is irrelevant and every form of male/female differentiation has been removed.

There exist so-called "filters" that have the ability to prevent access to sexually explicit materials, including those materials that have been located inadvertently. These same groups have consistently opposed the filters, and have argued for laws that make it unlawful for schools or libraries to install the filters. It is sad that the technology to overcome the ability of the filter to screen out pornography is ahead of the "filter" technology itself. Many computer software stores actually carry software that will overcome the filter. To be effective, a filter has to be continually updated. Parents who have once installed a filter and then assumed that the necessary precaution has been taken would be well advised to constantly monitor the effectiveness of the filter.

For parents who wish to be assured that their children are not being exposed to pornography on the Internet, nor being seduced by the predatory pedophiles who use the Internet to find unsuspecting children, there is only one certain solution to the issue of protecting their children. They must ever be on guard to know what their child is doing on the Internet at home, at school, or at the library. How to effectively "be on guard" depends upon the home, the child, and the circumstances. One thing that is certain is that parents cannot expect either the school or the public library to protect their children from the dangers that are involved with the Internet.

In many communities throughout the country determined parents have required the school board and the local governing authority for the public library to place "filters" on the computers in these institutions. This certainly is a very minimum of what any concerned community of parents should require. There are available from a number of credible sources around the country suitable petitions and standard resolutions to be adopted by local school boards and library boards or governing councils to require that these "filters" be installed and utilized.

CHAPTER TEN

THE SURVIVAL
OF THE REPUBLIC

———————

Most people who knew me assumed that my anti-pornography efforts were simply an extension of my religious convictions. To a limited extent that was an accurate assumption, but in fact my primary motivation in fighting against pornography was my political philosophy regarding freedom. Stated succinctly, I believe very strongly that the greatest threat to our political freedom is the loss of moral values. To put it in a positive sense, the most vital factor in the preservation of our freedom and liberty is our people's respect for moral values and their commitment to them. They are the vital foundation upon which rests our ability to obtain and maintain individual political freedom.

No array of nuclear armed guided missiles, no legion of armed warriors, no tyrant or dictator, no outlandish political philosophy holds anywhere near the capacity to destroy our nation and our legacy of freedom that the insidious spread of pornography among the American people does. As a public official I was often accosted with the question "What concern is it of yours whether or not someone wants to indulge in pornography? That is their own business and should not be a matter of concern for the government." The most direct answer to that question was given by a British jurist, Lord Patrick Devlin, who as Chairman of a Royal Commission on the issue of pornography in the United Kingdom wrote as follows: "an established morality is as necessary as good government to the welfare of society. Societies disintegrate from within more frequently than they are broken up by external pressures. There is disintegration when no common morality is observed and history shows that the loosening of moral bonds is often the first stage of disintegration, so that society is justified in taking the same steps to preserve its moral code as it does to preserve its government and other essential institutions. *The suppression of vice is as much the law's business as the suppression of subversive activities"* (*The Enforcement of Morals*, Oxford: Oxford University Press, 1968; emphasis added).

Among the current cadre of revisionist historians in our academies of learning it is highly popular to denigrate America's founding fathers and to ascribe to them motives and behavior that makes their sacrifice in the founding of the Republic nothing more than a self-serving effort for personal economic benefit. Yet all history must search in vain to find at one time in one place a more remarkable and brilliant assembly of men. They understood the relationship of moral values to freedom. If they were living with us today their voices would be raised in continual warning that the ultimate result of our continued downward spiral of moral values will be the loss of our personal and political freedom.

Their rationale was very clear and concise. To be free of tyrannical government a people must be willing to be governed by the supremacy of law. The greater the commitment to the supremacy of law the greater their ability to be self-governing under law and hence the less the need to force them into a particular pattern of behavior. Edmund Burke wrote of this fundamental political truth as follows: "Men are qualified for civil liberty in exact proportion to their disposition to put moral chains upon their own appetites—in proportion as their love of justice is above their rapacity; in proportion as their soundness and sobriety of understanding is above their vanity and presumption; in proportion as they are more disposed to listen to the counsel of the wise and good, in preference to the flattery of knaves. Society cannot exist, unless a controlling power upon the will and appetite is placed somewhere; and the less of it there is within, the more there must be without. It is ordained in the eternal constitution of things, that men of intemperate minds cannot be free. Their passions forge their fetters" (*The Works of the Right Honorable Edmund Burke,* comp. Humphrey Milford, Oxford: Oxford University Press, 1907).

Of a more recent vintage Walter Berns, in a classic essay defending the justification and need in society for the use of responsible censorship in order to protect society from the ultimate result of eroded moral values, has written: "Such was the argument made prior to the twentieth century, when it was generally understood that democracy, more than any other form of government, requires self-restraint, which it would inculcate through moral education and impose on itself through laws, including laws governing the manner of public amusements. It was the tyrant who would usually allow the people to indulge themselves. Indulgence of the sort we are now witnessing did not threaten his rule, because his rule did not depend on a citizenry of good character. Anyone can be ruled by a tyrant, and the more debased his subjects, the safer his rule" (From an essay entitled: *"Democracy, Censorship, and the Arts"* (quoted by Victor Cline in *Where Do You Draw The Line?* [Provo: Brigham Young University Press, 1974], p. 31).

The only way to have a nation whose people can be self-governing under the rule of law is if that people have embraced the moral values that will instill within them the self-discipline to honor and obey the law. In our day we have seen the near total failure of democratic self-government in Russia because the people as a whole had no common heritage of morality. Thus the smooth execution of civil and social functions we take for granted could not be accomplished in the Russian experience.

Our freedom is totally dependent upon our commitment to moral values. Pornography destroys the ability to be self-disciplined through commitment to morality. Thus the spread of pornography is a direct threat to the freedom and liberty that has come to us because of our legacy of Christian-based moral values.

Former President Woodrow Wilson once said: "Our liberties are safe until the memories and experience of the past are blocked out, and the Mayflower with its band of Pilgrims forgotten; until the public school system has fallen into decay, and the nation into ignorance" (*Great Quotations,* ed. George Seldes [New York: L. Stuart, 1960], p. 604).

The "ignorance" of which Woodrow Wilson spoke is now one of the most critical weaknesses of our social fabric. Our schools no longer teach, as once they did, the vital relationship between moral values and the legacy of freedom that has come to us from the past.

It is my conviction that the existence and acceptance of pornography in our culture constitutes the greatest single threat to our political freedom and liberty. As the presence of pornography grows and the resistance to it erodes, the essential and fundamental requirements for enduring as a free society are continually undermined and finally destroyed. Our founding fathers knew this and several of them predicted that if the time should come when the American people became "corrupted" in their moral values they would soon lose their freedom.

Robert Bork, whom we quoted in chapter 4, affirmed this truth as follows:

> It is possible to argue for censorship . . . on the ground that in a republican form of government where the people rule, it is crucial that the character of the citizenry not be debased. By now we should have gotten over the liberal notion that its citizens' characters are none of the business of government. The government ought not try to impose virtue, but it can deter incitements to vice. "Liberals have always taken the position," the late Christopher Lasch wrote, "that democracy can dispense with civic virtue. According to this way of thinking, it is liberal institutions, not the character of citizens, that make democracy work." He cited India and Latin America as proof that formally democratic institutions are not enough for a workable social order, a proof that is disheartening as the conditions in parts of large American cities approach those of the Third World. (Robert Bork, *Slouching Towards Gomorrah* [New York: Regan Books, 1996], pp. 141–42)

The man who is properly called the father of the Constitution, James Madison, wrote in the fifty-first Federalist Paper as follows: "We base this whole experiment (referring to the Constitution) on man's ability to be governed by law."

In stating that conviction Madison was reflecting the tremendous influence upon the founding fathers of the philosophy of John Locke, who in his *Treatise on Law and Freedom* wrote as follows: "The end of law is not to abolish or restrain but to preserve and enlarge freedom. For in all the states of created beings capable of laws, where there is no law there is no freedom. For liberty is to be free from restraint and violence from others; which cannot be where there is no law; and is not, as we are told, the liberty for every man to do what he lists—for who could be free when every other man's humor might domineer over him?"

When the Constitutional convention was finished a citizen of Philadelphia asked Benjamin Franklin: "Dr. Franklin, what kind of government have you given to us?" To which Franklin responded: "A Republic, if you can keep it."

The citizen then asked; "What do you mean, 'if we can keep it'?"

Then said Franklin: "This Republic, which we have given you with this constitution, will end in despotism, as other forms of government have done before it, when the people become so corrupt that they are incapable of any other form of government."

The statements of many other of the founding fathers reinforce and confirm the words of Madison and Franklin.

What the founding fathers of the American Republic also noted was that a people could not be governed by law unless they possessed the moral values that would enable them to exercise the self-discipline to obey the law. George Washington, in his "Farewell Address" stated:

> Of all the dispositions and habits which lead to political prosperity, religion and morality are indispensable supports. In vain would that man claim the tribute of patriotism, who should labor to subvert these great pillars of human happiness, these firmest props of the duties of men and citizens. The mere politician, equally with the pious man, ought to respect and cherish them. A volume could not trace all their connexions (sic) with private and public felicity. . . . And let us with caution indulge the supposition that morality can be maintained without religion. Whatever may be conceded to the influence of refined education on minds of peculiar structure, reason and experience both forbid us to expect that national morality can prevail to the exclusion of religious principle.
>
> It is substantially true that virtue or morality is a necessary spring of popular government. (*Basic American Documents:* pp. 108–9)

W. Cleon Skousen has been one of the Latter-day Saints' most intense scholars of America's legacy of freedom. In his monograph,

"The Secret to America's Strength, The Role of Religion in the Founding Fathers' Constitutional Formula," Dr. Skousen quotes from the Frenchman Alexis de Tocqueville, considered one of the most perceptive analysts of the American legacy of freedom. Said Dr. Skousen:

> De Tocqueville points out that "In France I had almost always seen the spirit of religion and the spirit of freedom marching in opposite directions. But in America I found they were intimately united" (*Democracy in America,* vol. 1, p. 319). He then points out that the early American colonists "brought with them into the New World a form of Christianity which I cannot describe than by styling it a democratic and republican religion. This contributed powerfully to the establishment of a republic and a democracy in public affairs; and from the beginning, politics and religion contracted an alliance which has never been dissolved" (Ibid, p. 311).
>
> However, he emphasized the fact that this religious undergirding of the political structure was a common denominator of moral teachings in different denominations and not the political pressure of some national church hierarchy. Said he: "The sects (different denominations) that exist in the United States are innumerable. They all differ in respect to the worship which is due to the Creator, but they agree in respect to the duties which are due from man to man. Each sect adores the Deity in its own peculiar manner, but all sects preach the same moral law in the name of God."
>
> It was astonishing to de Tocqueville that liberty and religion could be combined in such a balanced structure of harmony and good order. He wrote: "The revolutionists of America are obliged to profess an ostensible respect for Christian morality and equity, which does not permit them to violate wantonly the laws that oppose their designs. . . . Thus, while the law permits the Americans to do what they please, religion prevents them from conceiving and forbids them to commit, what is rash or unjust" (Op cit. p. 316). (Skousen, "The Secret to America's Strength," The Freeman Institute, May 1981, pp. 5–6)

The French historian, Francois Pierre Giuzot, while visiting the United States, asked James Russell Lowell, "How long will the American Republic endure?" Lowell pondered the question and then answered: "As long as the ideas of the men who founded it continue to be dominant."

On the entrance to the National Archives in Washington is a quote taken from one of Shakespeare's plays. It reads: "The past is prologue." The lesson is obvious and simple. The best way to obtain understanding of the present is to understand the past. The surest indicator of the future is to look at the present in light of the past. The present will dictate the future, and the attitudes, values, and virtues of the present will be the most determinative factors influencing the future.

The author Taylor Caldwell, in her marvelous work on the life of Cicero, *A Pillar of Iron,* attributes to Cicero as a member of the Roman Senate the following prophetic utterance regarding the ultimate destiny of the Roman empire: "The daily spectacle of atrocious acts has stifled all feeling of pity in the hearts of men. When every hour we see or hear of an act of dreadful cruelty we lose all feeling of humanity. Crime no longer horrifies us. We smile at the enormities of our youth. We condone passion, when we should understand that the unrestrained emotions of men produce chaos. Once we were a nation of self-control and austerity, and had a reverence for life and justice. This is no longer true. We prefer our politicians, particularly if they swagger with youth and are accomplished jesters and liars. We love entertainment, even in law, even in government. Unless we reform our fate is terrible" (*A Pillar of Iron* [New York: Doubleday, 1965], p. 322).

It would be difficult to give a more accurate description of the peril we now face than was contained in these words attributed to Cicero.

The certainty that the "past is prologue" has not been lost on the great teachers of history. Dame Edith Hamilton, in her work *The Greek Way to Western Civilization,* commented with sadness on the fact that our modern schools have by and large ceased the study of the Greek and Roman worlds, and how their magnificent civilizations came to a dismal end. She said: "Is it rational that now, when the young people may have to face problems harder than we faced . . . we are giving up the study of how the Greeks and Romans prevailed magnificently in a barbaric world; the study too, of how the triumph ended, how a slackness and softness finally came over them to their ruin? In the end, more than they wanted freedom, they wanted security, a comfortable life, and they lost all—security and comfort and freedom" (*The Greek Way to Western Civilization,* New York: New American Library, 1948).

There is another quote at the entrance of our national archives that is often repeated but apparently seldom believed. It is: "Eternal Vigilance Is the Price of Liberty."

In my youth I preferred reading actual history to novels or adventure mysteries. The ability to read what others had actually done inspired me much more than the fantasies of what people dreamed but never did. In that light I resolved that my life would be committed to doing whatever I could to preserve the legacy and heritage that had come to me through the sacrifice of my fathers. I found a passage in the New Testament that became a personal motto. Written by James the apostle, it reads: "But he who looks unto the perfect law, the law of liberty, and perseveres, being no hearer that forgets but a doer that acts, he shall be blessed in all his doing" (James 1:25, Revised Standard Version).

A lesson that I had learned early in my career as a lawyer and a politician was that if you believed a principle to be true and defended it with knowledge, more often than not those who were contemptuous of your values would not be able to overcome the power of your conviction.

Some years ago I was invited to be a guest at a dinner in Washington, D.C., in honor of a close friend who was retiring from a position as a member of the president's cabinet. During the dinner I sat at the same table with several individuals who held positions in the higher echelons of the federal government. Several of the "couples" at the table had been living together without the formality of marriage or the expectation of any permanency or exclusivity to their sexual partnership. Indeed, for several the current relationship was just one of those necessary stages in their career enhancement among the Washington crowd who traffic in influence with key government figures.

Early in the discussion it became apparent that to the majority of the people with whom I dined that evening I was regarded as somewhat irresponsible, even immoral, because my wife and I were the parents of ten children. Without rancor I responded with the comment that it seemed to me that the total absence of any permanency of commitment, loyalty, or fidelity in the "convenience relationships" of the individuals who openly paraded and espoused their current cohabitation dramatically represented how much our society had changed in the values that were once deemed the essential fabric of the American Republic. I noted as a "politician" that the essential political unit of the Republic was the family unit, and that those who demeaned the honored status of the family could be regarded as being numbered among the current crop of radical militants seeking to overturn the Constitution

My comments were not intended to be belligerent as much as to make certain that the hearers understood without any doubt what my attitude was toward their contempt for that which traditionally had been the key element to the nation's triumph over challenges of the past. The participants decided to change the subject, but they also showed in their demeanor that in their hearts they knew I was right, even if outwardly they had scorn and contempt for the values I espoused.

Thus, with regard to my confrontations with the apologists for pornography, I soon found that to be forthright and totally committed to the values of righteousness were ever the strongest, most effective weapons that I possessed. When one was apologetic or halfhearted in defense of truth and virtue the enemy sensed weakness and would relentlessly increase their attack.

In the ancient world there were those who understood the reality that the critical need for "eternal vigilance" was the price to be paid for preserving our liberty. One of these was Pericles, who was quoted by Thucydides in his history of the Peloponnesian War as saying: "We do not say that a man who ignores politics is a man who minds his own business. We say that he has no business being here at all."

Ignorance and apathy have ever been the enemies of freedom, the tools by which a legacy of liberty was soon lost. Samuel Adams once wrote to his son: "The liberties of our country, the freedom of our civil constitution, are worth defending at all hazards; and it is our duty to defend them against all attacks. We have received them as a fair inheritance from our worthy ancestors; they purchased them for us with toil and danger and at the expense of treasure and blood, and transmitted them to us with care and diligence. It will bring an ever-lasting mark of infamy on the present generation, enlightened as it is, if we should suffer them to be wrested from us by violence without a struggle, or be cheated out of them by the artifices of false and designing men."

Clarence B. Randall noted: "The characteristic of a free society is that there is no privilege that is not counter-balanced by an appropriate responsibility."

In the battles against the pornographers I often encountered a county prosecutor or law enforcement officer who would say words to this effect: "Yes, I could do more to get rid of pornography in our community, but no one cares. I seldom get a phone call or a letter complaining about the presence of a pornographic motion picture or bookstore. If I had to rely on public awareness and concern to justify my efforts in combating pornography we would never make an arrest."

The price of our ignorance and apathy will indeed be a most costly one. Over a hundred years ago in Great Britain Queen Victoria celebrated her diamond jubilee, commemorating sixty-five years of her leadership of the British people. The Pax Britannica that had prevented major war in Europe for almost a century was in full flower. For the great Jubilee, which saw an unmatched gathering of world rulers in London, most British poets and writers penned effusive praise about Britain's might and glory. Only one saw through the future haze to the reality of what might come to pass unless the lessons of the past were reaffirmed among the British people. That one was Rudyard Kipling, whose somber "Recessional" became a classic gloomy prophecy that all too soon was to be fulfilled. In one verse which seems so applicable to the American nation of today he wrote as follows:

> Far-called our navies melt away;
> On dune and headland sinks the fire.
> Lo, all our pomp of yesterday
> Is one with Nineveh and Tyre!

Judge of the nations, spare us yet,
Lest we forget, lest we forget."

By what remarkable arrogance do we presume to defy history's past lessons and Almighty God's judgment? By what cowardice or apathy do we turn our backs away from the challenge to our survival—and the duty to arise and meet that challenge?

A substantial portion of the television industry insists on the right to profit from obscenity pornography, prostitution, and deviancy Is the pseudo-sophistry of our entertainment industry really going to persuade this nation to accept these perversions as evidence of greatness instead of what they really are, the fruits of inner decay?

This is not only a moral issue; it is also an issue that affects the survival of the Republic. It begins with the individual and the family, extends to the neighborhood and the community, and ultimately attacks the nation as a whole. Why should we tolerate these perversions that are slowly but with certainty destroying the legacy and heritage that gave our nation its birth and sustained its life?

During the time that I was actively involved in the fight against pornography I was constantly accused of bigotry, or pseudo-piety, or seeking to impose my own narrow-minded morality upon the body politic. It was expected that in this endeavor one would be accused and belied. That was to be accepted as part of the great battle against evil. Ever and always we had to endure the rhetorical tactic that says if you cannot refute the message, then attack the messenger. The fact remained that there had to be a confrontation with those who would market degeneracy to our youth, whose commercialization of filth was ready to destroy homes and families wherever it could gain an entry into the inner sanctum.

The invidious enticement of pornography will addict and destroy even the most solidly grounded individual. Without the protective strength of a home and community truly mobilized in opposition to this evil, far too many youth will be quickly enticed into its destructive allure. Once that happens they not only lose the ability to stand faithful and strong in defense of truth and virtue, they become participants in the great demise of our national heritage. We must be prepared to wage a continuing battle against any further compromise with the pornographers in the legislatures, the Congress, the courts, and the schools. To allow the secret combination of the pornographers, the motion picture producers, the slick magazine publishers, and their ever present advocates, the ACLU, to succeed would be an eternal indictment for which there could be no honorable forgiveness.

For the Latter-day Saint, the survival of the American Republic is an essential part of his religious responsibility. The Constitution of the United States is a divinely revealed document intended by the Lord to be a vital factor in preparing the earth for the Savior's return. One cannot in ignorance or apathy fulfill that mandate to preserve the Constitution and the institutions of our liberty.

CHAPTER ELEVEN

"WE SEEK AFTER THESE THINGS"

My son Joe was the president of his high school senior class, an All-State football player, a varsity wrestler and soccer player. With all of these accomplishments he never showed any of the attitudes or behavioral patterns of conceit or arrogance. He was ever and always a very soft-spoken, quiet young man who tried to do his best at whatever the issue before him might involve. I can never remember a moment when we, as his parents, were concerned about his trustworthiness or his commitment to the values and the standards that were understood to be a part of our family.

Our home is in Utah. I would doubt that any similar-sized area in the country had the density of Latter-day Saints per capita that our city had at the time of which I write. By actual residence count ninety-two percent of the families living in our ward boundaries were LDS.

Down the hill from our home was a "neighborhood" movie theater. I have forgotten how the circumstance arose, but one evening Joe and I found ourselves with a free evening and we decided to attend the theater to see a movie that was of interest to both of us. The movie had a PG rating, so we assumed that some "action" scenes contained in the film had produced that rating. (Given my personal awareness of the duplicity of the rating system I have to admit being guilty of a severe lapse of good sense in placing any confidence in the published rating.)

As we sat in the theater awaiting the beginning of the show we grected a number of friends from our neighborhood and from the high school that Joe attended. To our knowledge at least eighty percent of the people in the theater whom we recognized were known to us to be members of the Church. It seems probable that eighty percent of all the patrons in the theater were Church members.

Early into the feature film an explicitly sexual encounter took place between the lead male and female actors. As soon as it began both Joe and I became uncomfortable, and as I was preparing to stand up Joe leaned over to me and said, "Should we leave?" We both stood and walked out into the foyer of the theater. When we were in front of the candy counter I asked Joe to wait for a while and I stood watching the exits from the theater into the lobby. Not one other person came out of the theater.

As we drove to our favorite ice cream store (a consolation alternative for the disappointment at not being able to enjoy the film) I posed to Joe the question: "Why do you suppose we were the only ones to leave the theater? Is there something about what we saw there that would justify remaining? And if there was not, why did not others who share our same values, and presumably the same commitment to those values, also leave?"

Joe pondered for some time before he gave his response. "I guess they just weren't bothered by it."

"Why weren't they bothered by it?" I said. "You and I certainly were uncomfortable watching something that we knew to be contrary to what we know to be right. Why didn't anyone else sense the same discomfort that we did?"

Joe was never happy with being cross-examined like this, but he accepted the challenge to think through what had just happened. Our ice cream was now on the table in front of us, so he could relax a bit and ponder the question. It took several minutes for him to formulate his response.

"Well," he finally said, "for our family there is no question that you and Mom would consider what was happening on the screen as not acceptable in our personal behavior, therefore it was not acceptable as our entertainment. I guess everyone else there believed it was okay."

Now I was the one who had to ponder what struck me as a profound insight. "Everyone else there believed that it was okay." Joe was absolutely right. The essential issue in all of this was the definition of what one "really believed."

My wife and I had never expressly told our children that the type of physical intimacy that appeared on the screen of that theater was "unacceptable in their personal behavior," though indeed it most certainly was unacceptable. How then did Joe know that because of what we "really believed" we would expect him to leave the theater when such a presentation appeared on the screen? I posed that question, along with another: "Would you have left if I had not been there?"

He answered the second question first with an unhesitating "Yes, I would have. I have done it in the past and I would have done it tonight. Remember, I was the one who said we should leave."

Now we came to what I really wanted to understand. How had he learned "to really believe" what standard we would expect him to apply in a situation like this?

Joe smiled, and then he began to recite something that we had taught our children repeatedly during family nights. In fact, there was often an unannounced contest that paid a dollar to each one who could recite it. Joe began, "Would you judge the lawfulness of pleasure, take this rule. . . . "

Before my wife and I had welcomed our first child into our family we had lived in Washington, D.C., where I attended law school. In the Chevy Chase Ward of Maryland we were both involved as teachers in priesthood meeting and Sunday School with the teenagers of the ward. While on my mission in England I had found a memorable quote contained in a letter written to John Wesley by his mother while he was a student at Cambridge University. Both my wife and I had used that quote frequently as we taught the youth in the Chevy Chase Ward. As our own children came along we continued to use it in our family night lessons.

Nearly three hundred years ago young John Wesley arrived at Cambridge University. There he found himself confronted with "temptations" that he did not know how to judge as to their acceptability. He wrote his mother a letter in which he asked her to write to him and to give him a list of what activities were "acceptable" and

which ones were not. In her return letter his mother gave the following instruction to her son. She told him there was no such list, and
then she said:

> Would you judge the lawfulness of pleasure, take this rule:
> Whatever weakens your reason,
> Whatever increases the authority of your body over your mind,
> Whatever impairs the tenderness of your conscience,
> Whatever takes away your relish for things spiritual,
> Whatever obscures your sense of God,
> That is sin to you, no matter how innocent it may seem in itself.

Joe smiled as he recited the quote, and then said with a grin so
uniquely his own, "Do I get a dollar?" He got his dollar, but a million
dollars would not have paid for the feeling in my heart as my son, "in
whom I was well pleased," looked across that table and assured me
that as a father I had not failed. Through many family nights our children had come to understand "what we really believed" even though
we had never made a "list" of those things they could accept and
those that they could not. We had taught them some principles in
which we believed, and they in turn had learned to apply those principles to the circumstances with which they were confronted in life.

What Joe and I observed that night caused us to question whether
all of our friends and neighbors who were present really did believe
in what they had so often recited in the thirteenth article of faith.
Every LDS child who graduates from Primary can recite the thirteenth article of faith, which says: "if there is anything virtuous,
lovely, of good report, or praiseworthy, we seek after these things."

What appeared on the screen that night was anything but "virtuous,
lovely, of good report, or praiseworthy." By any criteria, if anyone in
that theater believed that we as a Church are committed to seek after
things that are "virtuous, lovely, of good report or praiseworthy," then
we would have expected them not to remain in that theater.

But our problem is that we teach our children to recite words
without knowing what they really mean, without having made a personal commitment to live and abide by those words in our conduct
and actions. To "believe" something is to be committed to it, to

govern our conduct and our values in harmony with what we say we "believe." The overwhelming majority of our fellow Latter-day Saints who were in the theater that night could recite the thirteenth article of faith, but to what extent did they believe it?

How had Joe and his siblings come to believe in the advice from John Wesley's mother that we had taught them to recite? On a variety of occasions my wife and I have been asked by friends to outline for them how we "taught" our children. These questions have come to us repeatedly because we are the parents of ten children, who, to the best of our knowledge, have lived their lives in total harmony with the principles of the gospel of Christ as they have learned them in our home. On one occasion when a group of friends were visiting in our home that question was raised. At that moment one of our married sons, Matthew, with children of his own, happened to be in our home. We invited him to come into the room and respond to the questions being asked of us by our guests.

When the question was posed again he paused, and then said: "In our home there was never any doubt about what our parents believed was right and wrong—but there was never any attempt to force us to behave in a certain way. We were free to follow our own wishes, but there was never any doubt about what Mom and Dad expected of us if we wanted to please them."

An example of that was our teaching of our children regarding the Sabbath day. My wife and I felt strongly that most television on Sunday was antagonistic to the Lord's intention and desires concerning the Sabbath day. We particularly disapproved of watching sporting events on Sunday television. Both of us simply refused to be present in the family room if someone in the family had a sports event on TV on Sunday.

We never told our children that they could not or should not watch television on Sunday. Rather, we taught them the principle that the Sabbath day was a day to worship, to remember the Lord in fasting and prayer for His goodness to us, and to strengthen our bonds as a family unit. Then we showed our children by our conduct that we really "believed" what we had taught them. If someone in the family felt justified in watching a Sunday football game, that was their choice.

As other questions were asked of our son, he made one other comment. He said: "We were free to do what we wanted—but if we did something to displease our parents, their disappointment was very very painful to us. Free agency didn't leave you free from the stern look in Dad's eyes that made it clear he did not appreciate the behavior."

I do not recite this to suggest that if in other homes there is a different standard regarding the Sabbath day they are or are not in harmony with the will of the Lord. The purpose in reciting the above experience was to demonstrate how our children came to "believe" in a gospel principle that we felt was vital to their lives.

First of all, we taught them what the principle or commandment might be. Then, by our example and our conduct, we taught them to recognize that we really "believed" what we had taught them. If one "believes in something," then there is a certain value attached to the principle or concept which is the object of the belief. When a visible value is attached to anything there is a discernable measure of the extent of belief. We demonstrate by how we live the "value" that we attach to those things in which we say we "believe." No matter what I may say about the Sabbath day, what I really believe about the Sabbath day is reflected in what I do on the Sabbath day.

This same method applies to any other gospel concept, principle, or practice. Parents cannot teach loyalty to or acceptance of the thirteenth article of faith and its confident assertion that we seek after that which is "virtuous, lovely, of good report, or praiseworthy" unless in their home and in their family life, those same principles govern that on which they spend their money or to which they commit their time. The most visible and tangible measure of value in our culture is our money. The second is our time. Where we spend our time and our money is that to which we attach the highest value. If we are unwilling to give our time or our money to a certain activity or object we obviously do not regard it as having much value to us. Our children see this and they instinctively know that in which we really believe by the value we place on it as reflected by the time and money we commit to it.

When Joe and I walked out of that theater we both demonstrated that the value we placed on things that were "virtuous, lovely, of good report, or praiseworthy" exceeded the cost of the admission ticket to the theater. When my wife and I excused ourselves from the family room when what was on the TV screen was inconsistent with our commitment to the Sabbath day, we were teaching our children that to which we attached the higher value. Our Sabbath day values were not consistent with sporting events or even weekday television programming. Honoring the Lord was too precious to us to waste the Sabbath day in doing something inconsistent with that which would please Him.

What does all of this have to do with the issue of the increasing presence of pornography in our culture? In today's high-tech world the only defense against the intrusion of pornography into our homes and the lives of our children is for parents to teach their children to really believe in the value of truth and virtue. Quite obviously the critical issue is being able to commit ourselves to what we really believe. Most people do not allow themselves to become involved with pornography without having previously compromised their loyalty to that which is "virtuous, lovely, of good report, or praiseworthy." Or, if you wish, go back to the letter to John Wesley from his mother. Can you ask yourself at any given moment if that in which you are engaged meets the criteria she set forth? Can you ask yourself, "Is what I am doing something that will:

> . . . weaken my reason,
> increase the authority of my body over my mind,
> impair the tenderness of my conscience,
> take away my relish for things spiritual,
> obscure my sense of God?"

If the answer to any of these questions is yes, then the chances are that for you that activity is indeed "sinful," no matter how innocent it may seem in itself.

To state the issue in the affirmative, ask "Is what I am doing something that is 'virtuous, lovely, of good report, or praiseworthy?'" If it is not, then the chances are that for me "that is sinful, no matter how innocent it may seem in itself."

Most of the motion pictures now produced (and apparently

patronized by Latter-day Saints) are not virtuous, lovely, of good report, or praiseworthy. Most of the television programs Latter-day Saints spend their time watching do not increase their reason, do not increase the authority of their spirits over their bodies, do not increase the tenderness of their conscience, do not increase their sense of things spiritual, and do not increase their awareness of the presence of God. If that is true, are not such things "sinful" insofar as the LDS faithful are concerned? Is it not the failure to abide by that in which we say we believe that is diminishing our relish for things spiritual?

It is my personal conviction that in this matter we are not properly observing the mandate given to us of the Lord, because in fact we are not "a peculiar people" in our choice of that in which we really believe. Abstaining from tobacco, tea and coffee, and alcohol hardly qualifies us as a truly "peculiar" people. Patronizing entertainments that are patently antagonistic to that in which we assert we really believe, extolling individual entertainers, athletes, and politicians whose personal lives reject all that we are supposed to honor and hold in high esteem—this tells our children what we really value. When we give our time, our money, and our loyalty to those and to that which are out of harmony with true loyalty to gospel principles and doctrines, we show our children and the world that in which we "really believe."

How much longer we will be able to "live in the world" without refusing to be "of the world" is highly problematical. The constant erosion of any sense of dignity, virtue, or loveliness in worldly arts, entertainments, and literature make it clear that soon the Latter-day Saints will have to choose "whom they will serve." Making that choice in harmony with the gospel will require sacrificing many of the "pleasures" of the world. As the now thin line between obscenity, carnality, and pornography, and acceptable forms of amusement and entertainment finally disappears, many will need to find their way out of the "mists of darkness" into which they have been seduced, if they are once again to grasp the iron rod.

Would you judge the lawfulness of pleasure, take this rule:
Whatever weakens your reason,

Whatever increases the authority of your body over your mind,
Whatever impairs the tenderness of your conscience,
Whatever takes away your relish for things spiritual,
Whatever obscures your sense of God,
That is sin to you, no matter how innocent it may seem in itself.

We believe that "if there is anything virtuous, lovely, or of good report or praiseworthy, we seek after these things."

CHAPTER TWELVE

THE POWERS
OF DARKNESS

———————

I once watched how venomous snakes are "milked" of their venom to be used for medical treatments. The technician dealing with the snake did so with the greatest possible deference for the poison contained in the snake's fangs. Carefully and meticulously he maintained control over the snake's ability to free its head long enough for what could be a fatal strike with its fangs. The image and the memory of that technician "milking" the serpent of its venom remained vividly imprinted in my mind.

From the day that I decided to fight against pornography, this Satanically inspired spiritual and emotional poison, I had ever regarded pornography as just that—a venomous snake that could only be handled with the greatest respect for its poisonous power. I did so, confident that I could remain untarnished by what I had to see in order to engage the enemy in court and in the legislative chamber.

Notwithstanding all of my precautions, however, there came a time when I sensed a darkness in my soul. I never became "involved" with the behavior depicted in pornography, nor did I ever seek to act out the pathetic and vile behavior that pornography induces. But there were times when I had to spend several hours a day, or even all day for several days, viewing the pornographic materials that were the subject of our legislative or judicial battles. By constantly reminding myself of the perversion of what I was observing, and the poisonous nature of its content, I was confident that I could remain aloof from the insidious evils of pornography.

During one of the series of court battles that Clancy and I were pursuing there came a time when I was feeling alienated from that which was clean and wholesome. I found myself critical of my loved ones and judgmental of other members of the Church and of the leaders over me in the Church. I was negative in my heart toward such and to that which I knew was in harmony with the will of God. I experienced a sense of bitterness toward heaven and life, and an inner arrogance that began to manifest itself by contemptible thoughts about others. Prayer was not the meaningful moment of peaceful communion that it had been. The solace and the comfort that had accompanied my religious observances in the past were no longer being received.

I had never become involved in any of the deviant sexual conduct that pervades pornography. I had never compromised my covenants or violated the commandments about chastity. Yet a darkness had come into my mental and spiritual being. One day a comment from my wife made me stop and look more closely into my spiritual mirror. When I did so with an open mind and a sincere prayer to see "things as they really are" (Jacob 4:13), I became painfully aware of the "thick darkness" that had gathered around me.

Realizing that somehow the snake venom was getting into my system, with much fasting and prayer I sought some guidance. I was confused and very much concerned as to how and why I should be having this experience. Throughout the campaign for Proposition 18 I had felt a constant source of support and strength from the Spirit of the Lord. In the many years that I was attempting through other efforts, legislatively and in the courts, to fight against pornography, I had found the spiritual assurance that I was doing "the Lord's will." What was now happening was quite clear to me in the sense that the companionship of the Holy Ghost, which I had felt so keenly in the past, was withdrawn. Something was terribly wrong.

Should I give up the fight and abandon the effort? Did I dare go on, realizing that a spiritual darkness had come into my life? What to do and how to do it became terribly confusing to me.

I took my family to a Utah mountain resort for a vacation, and then returned to Los Angeles. I went to a man whose quiet dignity and humility had always been profoundly impressive to me, Brother

Myrthus Evans, the president of the Los Angeles Temple. We met in his office and I explained my problem and asked him if he could allow me to seek out, in the Temple, some relief from the "thick darkness" that was gathering around me. In addition, I needed to know whether I should continue the effort or retreat before my own defenses against pornography collapsed.

President Evans encouraged me to continue the efforts I was making, and he made it possible for me to spend an unusual amount of time in private worship in the Los Angeles Temple. Much fasting and prayer, and "laboring in the Spirit," continued for several weeks. Though I returned to my normal routine, I came back to the temple whenever I could spend two or three days in worship and vicarious service. There were several weeks during which I spent the majority of my time, including several all-night vigils, inside the temple. During the day I participated in the temple ordinances, and at night I remained in the president's private office.

I spent many hours in pondering, in solicitous appeals for understanding and cleansing. Eventually the effort had a miraculous effect. With a truly Christlike kindness President Evans gave counsel and encouragement. I spent much time searching the scriptures, and there found an answer as to what had happened to me. When that answer was found I began immediately to reverse the slow immersion into despair that had come to envelop my being.

Eventually the darkness departed, the memory of what I had been required to see and hear as part of my fight against pornography was mercifully taken away. A day came when I left the temple with a sense of having been cleansed. Though I continued the anti-pornography efforts for many years I was never again enveloped with the spiritual darkness—the absence of light and truth and the fruits of the Spirit—that had found its way into my soul.

What is perhaps more important, however, is that I came to understand something about the forces of evil that attend pornography that I had never previously understood. I had always associated the negative aspects of pornography with the deviant behavior that pornography induced. This included the vile sexual perversion, the various forms of sadomasochistic abuse and physical torture, the bestiality and the pedophilia. The ultimate perversion was, of course, the taking of human life as part of the pornographic experience.

Now, from my own experience of having to deal with the venom from the pornography serpent, I became aware of another form of pornography's ultimate power to destroy a soul. The involvement with pornography drives the "light of truth" away from our souls. Reading the scriptures awakened me to the profound truth that ever associated with all of our actions in life should be the Spirit of Christ and the ministry of the Holy Ghost. However, if what we say and think, and do, or if that with which we are associated is antagonistic to that Spirit, then the Spirit withdraws; and darkness, the abode of Satan, comes to replace it. Without my realizing what was happening, viewing pornographic materials had driven light and truth away from my being and left me in spiritual darkness. While dealing with the powers of darkness I had not taken the time to replenish the "light of truth" within my soul. Soon the darkness was suffocating in my life the manifestations of the Spirit of the Lord.

But I also learned another critical truth. If I could be redeemed from the effect of what I had seen and heard, so could anyone who really desired to be cleansed from the evil of pornography and who would go to the Lord with faith in His redeeming power. Dr. Victor Cline and other professional counselors have told me of the pitiful tragedies that accompanied those individuals who became their patients when addiction to pornography had overcome them. I mentioned previously the many occasions when a wife and mother would tearfully ask me to recommend someone to help them bring a husband lost in the mire of pornography back to the home and family that so much loved and needed him. The sense of helpless dismay that accompanied these requests was heartbreaking.

Many have been perplexed by King Benjamin's assertion that "the natural man is an enemy to God" (Mosiah 3:19). Basically, the natural man is one from whom the Spirit of Christ has departed because he loved darkness more than light. Mormon described the ultimate condition of the "natural man" to his son, Moroni, when he wrote regarding their own people:

And notwithstanding this great abomination of the Lamanites, it does not exceed that of our people. . . . For behold, many of the daughters of the Lamanites have they taken prisoners; and after depriving them of that which was most dear and precious above all things, which is chastity and virtue—

And after they had done this thing, they did murder them in a most cruel manner, torturing their bodies even unto death; and after they have done this, they devour their flesh like wild beasts, because of the hardness of their hearts. . . .

O the depravity of my people! They are without order and without mercy. . . .

And they have become strong in their perversion; and they are alike brutal, sparing none, neither old nor young; and they delight in everything save that which is good; . . . "

They are without principle and past feeling. (Moroni 9:9–10, 18–20)

Here we have the ultimate description of the fruits of pornography. When the Spirit of Christ, the "light of truth" (see D&C 84:45–46) is totally driven away from an individual, then the darkness that has filled that void conceives and produces the evils of which Mormon wrote to his son. It produces the mentality that would rape and murder a sweet little girl, that would take a young boy from his mother or grandmother and sexually abuse him, and then, without feeling or remorse, snuff out his life and dispose of his body.

It was also Mormon who wrote to his son that it is the Spirit of Christ within us which awakens us to "the light of truth."

"For behold, the spirit of Christ is given to every man, that he may know good from evil; . . . but whatsoever thing persuadeth men to do evil, and believe not in Christ, and deny him, and serve not God, then ye may know with a perfect knowledge it is of the devil. . . . And now, my brethren, seeing that ye know the light by which ye may judge, which light is the light of Christ. . . . I beseech of you, brethren, that ye should search diligently in the light of Christ that ye may know good from evil" (Moroni 7:16–19).

Paul wrote to the Corinthians that "[we] . . . are the temple of God. . . . If any man defile the temple of God, him shall God destroy; for the temple of God is holy, which temple ye are" (1 Corinthians 3:16–17). And in the Doctrine and Covenants the Lord tells us: "But if it [the temple] be defiled, I will not come into it . . . for I will not come into unholy temples" (D&C 97:17).

Thus both Alma and Amulek admonished their people: "[The Lord] doth not dwell in unholy temples" (Alma 7:21). "And this I know, because the Lord hath said he dwelleth not in unholy temples, but in the hearts of the righteous doth he dwell" (Alma 34:36).

That person who turns to pornography turns away from the light of truth that comes from the Spirit of Christ. He begins a journey into darkness which, if it continues long enough and far enough, reaches ultimate darkness, or outer darkness, where not even the Spirit of Christ can be found. That is when, as Mormon wrote to Moroni, that person reaches the ultimate depth of "depravity," and has become so strong in "perversions" that he is "past feeling," filled with brutality, "they are without principle."

That is why these individuals become capable of crimes against others that defy comprehension. One cannot begin to understand how one human can commit such brutality upon another. The answer very simply is, they have driven the "light of truth," the "Spirit of Christ" entirely out of their beings. Thus they display the worst elements of "the natural man," whom King Benjamin said "is an enemy to God." They are no longer able to sense pity, or remorse, or kindness, or tenderness of soul. As the prophet Mormon said, "they are without principle and past feeling." Whoever is about them are not fellow human beings but are merely objects to be abused, manipulated, used for whatever sordid pleasure can be derived, with no sense of remorse or sorrow for the suffering that may be inflicted, even if it leads to death.

With this understanding we can only wonder at what will happen to us when those pedophiles to whom the federal judge gave the right to read and embrace pornography daily while in their prison cells are finally released to the streets once again. The darkness within them that drove them to the commission of their unspeakable crimes against little children has never been replaced with the light of truth. In the midst of that darkness they have no feeling, no conscience, no restraint of the "natural man." All sources of light that would inhibit their evil conduct are now gone, the darkness is total, and how great that darkness has become!

He who willingly picks up the poisonous serpent of pornography cannot escape the venom that will soon be plunged into his life's blood by the serpent's fangs. The delusion that one can handle the poisonous serpent without getting bitten is the most foolish of all delusions. The Lord will not dwell in an "unholy" temple. To choose to allow the light of truth to be driven from our souls by the willful viewing of pornography is indeed the act of crucifying Christ on a spiritual cross of depravity. The end result is the misery that comes from the "dirt, disease, and death" that is ever the fruits of pornography.

When Joseph Smith was engaged in the translation of the Bible he came to the place in the book of Matthew where the Savior described how "evil spirits" find it possible to enter into our minds and hearts. Though the example is not exactly on point it does illustrate the principle involved. The Savior recited the account of the individual possessed of an evil spirit and from whom that evil spirit had been driven away by the power of the priesthood. But the Savior then noted that the individual now free from the evil spirit "speaketh against the Holy Ghost, then he [the evil spirit] saith, I will return into my house from whence I came out; and when he is come, he findeth him empty, swept and garnished; for the good spirit leaveth him unto himself" (JST Matthew 12:38).

Thus the Savior noted: "Then goeth he [the evil spirit], and taketh with himself seven other spirits more wicked than himself, and they enter in and dwell there; and the last state of that man is worse than the first" (Matthew 12:45).

We cannot see and hear—vicariously live and experience through motion pictures, videocassettes, and television—that which is of the antiChrist and expect to remain safely possessed of the Holy Ghost or the light of Christ. Could one imagine the prophets of the Lord watching a video or motion picture that extols violence and immorality, that makes a mockery of sacred things? Would you think the Lord could speak to you through a patriarch whose mind contained images from much of the current crop of PG, PG -13, and R-rated movies? Why should the Lord expect the rest of us to have any lesser standard than they?

I, who was so certain that the darkness could never enter into my being, awakened to the realization barely in time to "return to the light." The important thing to understand about that is that I never became involved with any of the behavior associated with pornography—I never became addicted to seeking out the materials that were more depraved and more vile than what I had previously seen. My motives and my use of the pornography were ever intended to be "wielding the sword of justice in defense of truth and virtue." Notwithstanding all of that, because I was too busy "doing good" I allowed myself to let the light of Christ within me grow dimmer and dimmer, not even knowing until the "thick darkness" had gathered about me how dim that light was becoming.

I shall be eternally grateful to President Myrthus Evans for his faith and confidence in me sufficient to allow me the sacred privilege of returning to the house of the Lord. Though I entered with more darkness than light in my soul, I emerged cleansed. I shall never forget the feeling of relief when that moment of purification seemed to be confirmed by the Spirit. I vowed that never again would I allow the light of truth to grow dim within the temple of my soul, and I have kept that solemn covenant by returning to the house of the Lord, ever clean, ever seeking in fasting and prayer that the "light of truth might grow brighter and brighter within me."

It is my solemn testimony to any who have become immersed in the mire of pornography that they too can "return to the light of Christ." The process of "seeing things as they really are," including oneself, is painful and soul searing. But it is a process which, when completed, allows one who has been one of the spiritual dead among the living to live spiritually again.

For many years after this experience I continued my efforts to oppose pornography. I still had to view the same materials in order to both testify and advocate before the courts and the public. But by my constantly seeking after the "light of Christ" and the presence and ministry of the Holy Ghost, the darkness was never able to overcome the light. Some of the ways in which I was able to maintain my spiritual commitment are too personal to recite here. Suffice it to say that there is no secret involved. Daily prayer and scripture study, frequent fasting, frequent renewal of covenants in the temple and on the Sabbath day were all a part of the means by which the darkness was dispelled by the light. Like the technician who milked the venomous snake, I was ever on guard against any possible mistake that could threaten my spiritual life. I have attempted without success to describe to others how it was done, but for some reason I can never adequately explain the process.

If any who should read these words has become imprisoned by addiction to pornography, has become surrounded by the mists of darkness, I witness to you with all of the intensity and fervor of which I am capable that you can return, you can yet be cleansed, if you will only desire through repentance, fasting, study of the scriptures, faith, worship, and prayer, to seek after that which is "virtuous, lovely, of good report, and praiseworthy."

CHAPTER THIRTEEN

"CHOOSE YOU THIS DAY WHOM YE WILL SERVE"

Earlier in this text I recited the incident that created the title to the monograph I later wrote about pornography on cable television, entitled, *To My Neutral Friends*. I had been in the Utah state capitol building meeting with elected officials about the issue of pornography on cable television. One of the members of the state legislature summarized his conclusion after listening to my presentation by simply saying, as he walked out of the room: "I'm really neutral on this issue. It doesn't affect me."

I hope anyone who has read this book now understands what a tragedy the attitude behind that statement represents. Pornography in our culture affects all of us. It has always been the source of misery to individuals, to families destroyed by its poisonous power, and to the communities in which its victims are found. The absurdity of the assertion that what one person chooses to do to entertain himself in the privacy of his own home is " no one's business but their own" should now be apparent.

Throughout the 1960s, the 1970s, and much of the 1980s my strategic objectives in the battle against pornography centered in the courts and the legislative chambers. The technologies that have created the ability to produce videocassette recordings and the Internet have basically eliminated the courts and the legislative process as viable factors in the effort to stem the tide of pornography. I do not wish to convey the thought that we should cease striving to enact laws against pornography's spread and assure their proper enforcement.

Clearly we must still strive for the enactment of laws that will deal with pornography. We must still petition our government officials to do all in their power to shield us from the gutter of slime that oozes from the pornographer's dens. But the key to victory over pornography lies neither in the courts nor in the legislative chamber. It lies within the home.

I hope that what is written herein helps people to better understand the danger of pornography, the power of this venomous serpent to inflict great pain and suffering, even to death. But more important, I hope that what I have written will strengthen the commitment of honorable men and women everywhere to resolve within themselves that there will be no surrender, no compromise with the "mists of darkness" that seek to destroy our culture, our civilization, and our destiny. The hour has come in which we must "draw the line" between ourselves and a society that is now so desensitized to filth that filth is not even recognized as such.

By "drawing the line" I do not mean to exclude ourselves from that society. I do suggest that we must confirm and coalesce our opposition to the surge of degeneracy that now permeates our entertainments, our literature, and our so-called arts. We can no longer casually endure (if not ultimately embrace) the continued downward spiral of our culture's art, literature, and entertainment into the abyss of vile perversion. As Joshua challenged Israel, so we must accept the challenge to "choose you this day whom ye will serve." As Christ taught so directly, "Ye cannot serve God and mammon." Latter-day Saints can no longer accept the false notion that it is possible to honor the covenants we have made, to be loyal to the Godhead who have revealed themselves to us, and at the same time participate, even in the role of a passive observer, in the practices all about us that are leading to greater and greater degeneracy.

The desensitizing effect of pornography has brought with its increased demand for graphic sex an equally abhorrent demand for graphic violence. Whether this violence is directly associated with sexual conduct or not, the purveyors of pornography have been all too willing to bring ultimate violence against other human beings into their products, be they motion pictures, magazines, music (if such it can be called), the electronic media in our homes, or live onstage presentations. Thus we are producing a generation who only have lost all sense of restraint or self-discipline in sexual conduct but also have become so thoroughly exposed to the inflicting of violent abuse upon other human beings that they have no ability to sense with empathy or remorse the cruelty or the evil of inflicting suffering upon another human being.

If the past thirty years of increased expansion of pornography's presence in our society continues at the same pace, what I see coming is such a breakdown of social order that society as we now know it will be torn apart. In a few years we shall see the structure of communities collapse because of the inability to maintain law and order. Violence and the disregard of the law will become so prevalent that neither the law enforcement agencies nor the courts will be capable of dealing with the magnitude of the civil disorder. When that occurs, the social order as we now know it will literally disintegrate. Those persons who still maintain some sense of civility will join together in self-defense and will turn to a form of vigilante law enforcement for self-protection.

As a public official and an attorney anti-pornography activist I was laughed at in 1972 when I predicted what would take place in the following twenty years. The only error of my prediction, though, was that it was too restrained. I did not foresee the technological developments of electronic communication via satellite and other means and what vastly greater opportunity for the pornographers such developments would make possible.

Unopposed, the pornographers will plunge our culture into an abyss of debauchery and mayhem that has never had a parallel in recorded history. Is there any way to effectively and successfully oppose this blight? Yes, there most certainly is. The complete answer to that question is not only law enforcement, legislatures, and the Congress, although we desperately need all of them to do more. The only way to effectively defeat the power of the pornographers is by the unyielding commitment of individual citizens, who create the commitment of individual families, who mobilize the commitment of individual communities.

The only reliable defense that parents now have to protect their children from the insidious evil of pornography is to have taught them from their infancy that pornography, like the bite of a venomous serpent, is certain death. The death is always spiritual, and sometimes physical as well. As an institution of learning, the Church can be helpful, but the Church alone can never be relied upon to win the battle. Given the innundation of pornography through so many media options it will take two dedicated parents, striving together with all of the capacity that the Holy Ghost can provide to them, and utilizing all of the support and guidance available through the Church, to protect their little ones from the "evil serpent." Anything less is, at best, a gamble with the odds against success, and at worst, the certainty of tragedy.

Does this mean that we should not continue the fight? Absolutely not! Across the country, the many honorable and dedicated people working through various worthy organizations in order to save our culture and our future deserve our support. We need to rally behind these organizations with our time, our money, and our talents. In addition to the obvious reasons why we should support them there is the critical need for our youth to see our determination to oppose this evil. They need to know that there are compelling reasons to suppress pornography. Our youth need to know that parents, leaders, and others whom they admire and to whom they turn for example and inspiration are not willing to accept defeat at the hands of these secret combinations of evil.

Our youth need to know how pornography is created and distributed by organized crime, the motion picture industry, the slick magazine publishers, and the myriad neurotic exhibitionists who have found an outlet for their sick minds through the Internet.

We have become too passive in accepting the standards of this world by which they of the world express their worship for "the God of this world." Either we must now "draw the line" between our principles, values, and standards, and theirs, or we must accept the ultimate reality that theirs will slowly but inevitably erode ours until our values disappear into oblivion. As it is, our youth sing their songs, laugh at their mockery of sacred things, and imitate their fashions. Often we adulate their heroes, more especially those whose personal lives represent a continued assault on everything that is "virtuous, lovely, or of good report or praiseworthy." We have become entangled in the coils of the evil one's subtlety of deceit until in far too many instances we have surrendered without acknowledging defeat.

The Savior and His prophets have warned us repeatedly that this would be a day of confusion about right and wrong, a day when even the "very elect" could be deceived (see Mark 13:22).

In 1969 I was deeply involved with the issues of drug abuse among California's youth. In my efforts to learn more about why young people were becoming involved with drugs I went to the state Youth Authority facility at Camarillo, California. There my mission was to interview a number of young people who were incarcerated for serious crimes associated with drug use. In preparing for the interviews I was given a stack of case files of various inmates from which I could choose the ones I wanted to interview. One of those files was of a teen-age girl. I noted in the file that her family were "active" members of The Church of Jesus Christ of Latter-day Saints.

As she and I met and discussed her involvement with drugs, she told me about her family. In every way her parents met the profile that one would expect of successful, even outstanding, parents. I found it hard to believe that someone from such a family would find herself in prison for a very serious crime associated with drug abuse. As the interview came to an end I asked her one final question. "Can you tell me why you are here? I do not mean the [crime for which she was convicted] but the more fundamental reason of what it was that allowed this to happen to you?"

She paused a moment, and then responded. "Yes, I can tell you that. The reason I am here is that the first time my mother and father ever really sat down and explained to me what they believed about right and wrong was when they came to visit me here in prison at Camarillo. All our lives they were too busy to share with me their deeper feelings—and then it was too late."

I fear that far too often Latter-day Saint parents are unwilling to let their children see them take a stand in favor of that which is "virtuous, lovely, of good report, or praiseworthy." They "feared man more than God," as the Savior said to Joseph Smith when he allowed Martin Harris to lose the initial Book of Mormon manuscript (see D&C 3:7). Too often parents are more committed to their children's popularity with their peers than they are to their eternal exaltation.

This is the end of my story. It began as a young husband and father in Glendale, California. In the course of my journey I have met on many occasions those who are the servants and legions of Satan. My eyes have seen the darkest, most abhorrent expressions of Satanic depravity. In courtrooms and legislative chambers we confronted the sophistry, the rhetoric, and the contempt for virtue and purity that ever come from the "prince of darkness."

After more than thirty years the situation is much worse than it was then. Thus, one must ask, what was the point of it all? For what purpose or benefit were all of the defeats? What good has come from being ridiculed by the media, from being falsely accused by those who had been my friends, from finding myself in peril of losing the light in my own life?

I have a deep conviction that through our efforts there was much good accomplished of which we may not be aware. But I also have a certain knowledge that in making the case for light and truth we helped dispel the powers of darkness. The time and effort was all worthwhile, if for no other reason than the fact that our testimony and our presence made it possible for the light to enter in and the darkness to be dispersed.

If the effort was worthwhile for no other reason, at least I can testify that I know whereof I speak about the abyss of darkness into which pornography will plunge the unwary. Pornography has only one final dividend: the mortal and eternal destruction of the soul. It will begin so softly, so subtly; and then step by step, day by day, the light of truth will grow just a little fainter, and the darkness become more pervasive. Finally, the powers of darkness will prevail, the light will have been driven away, and the lamentation of Mormon (see Moroni 9:8-14) for his people will be the epitaph for another lost soul.

The experiences set forth in this book have also taught me that there can be no compromise as to the responsibility of anyone who finds pornography in the life of someone near and dear. Whether it be a parent who discovers that a child has become involved with pornography, a spouse who finds pornography has found its way into the marriage partner's life, a bishop to whom a ward member admits having become entangled in this evil, or simply a friend who is a

brother or sister in the gospel, the course of action must be immediate and unequivocal. Pornography will destroy the spiritual life of
anyone who allows its darkness to take possession of his soul. The
process of redemption requires that the darkness be replaced with the
light, that the source of the poisonous evil be immediately shut off,
and that the endangered victim begin immediately to seek after that
which is "virtuous, lovely, of good report, or praiseworthy."

Clearly we are witnessing a great confrontation between light
and darkness. In a worldwide battleground the forces of Satan have
marshaled all of their powers to overcome the light. Because of the
electronic World Wide Web we have the ability to transmit instantaneously the visual images or the written language that describes anything to anyone anywhere on earth. Worldwide there are a hundred
thousand or more web sites that are dedicated solely to the presentation of pornography. Every expression of current values in the arts,
entertainment, music, and so forth conveys a constant theme of
opposition to all that is "virtuous, lovely, of good report, or praiseworthy."

Yet the technologies that have made it so easy to distribute that
which is vile have also made it possible to bring the voices of God's
prophets into every home on earth. In all of recorded history there
has never been so many who could and would do the Lord's work as
there are now. There has never been so much reason to find hope for
and have faith in the ultimate triumph of light and truth as there is
now. As the prophet Gordon B. Hinckley has repeatedly taught us,
we live in the most marvelous age in the history of the world. We
have every reason to rejoice in the promises that have been made to
those who qualify to be a "Zion" people. The mists of darkness need
never be allowed to ensnare our souls if we but heed Joshua's admo-
nition to "choose . . . this day whom ye will serve."

In a recently published book entitled *Rearing Righteous Youth of
Zion* (Bookcraft, 1997) BYU professors Brent L. Top and Bruce A.
Chadwick report on a survey done of LDS youth from three distinct
geographical areas. The survey endeavored to determine those factors that influenced most powerfully the lives of LDS youth, both for
good and for evil. It is surprising that some results of the survey can
be interpreted to indicate that in the areas of sexual promiscuousness

girls are having more difficulty than boys in dealing with certain temptations. Irrespective of that, however, in an article authored by the two professors that appeared in *Brigham Young Magazine,* summer of 1998, there were two very significant conclusions that the research seemed to justify.

The first conclusion is that geographic location does not seem to be a critical factor in the ability of LDS youth to resist temptation. The researchers noted: "Despite the arguments of some, our study showed that when raising teenagers, it doesn't really matter where the family lives. LDS teenagers in all three religious ecologies responded similarly to the questions about delinquency; only a few statistically significant differences surfaced in the analysis. It is easy to long for some sort of 'spiritual Shangri-la' but, unfortunately, there is no such place. The fortunate flip side of the coin is that it doesn't matter. In this study geography or religious ecology was insignificant. Teens face substantial peer pressure regardless of where they live, and, more important, they can be strong in the gospel wherever they reside. Truly, Zion is 'the pure in heart' (D&C 97:21), a spiritual condition rather than a geographical location" (Top and Chadwick, "Raising Righteous Children in a Wicked World," *Brigham Young Magazine,* Summer 1998).

The second significant conclusion of the study was that indeed the religious practices in the home constitute the greatest source of strength to a teenager seeking to resist the powers of evil. Said the researchers: "Another important result of the study was the identification of specific dimensions of religiosity that appear to make the biggest difference for youth. . . . The study showed private religious behavior, religious beliefs, and spiritual experiences to be highly correlated; hence, we grouped those three elements under one category: private religiosity. Private religiosity was the strongest predictor of delinquency among LDS teenagers: those youth who have internalized the gospel avoid delinquency to a greater extent than those youth who have not" (ibid).

Where do such personal religious convictions come into the lives of teenagers? Clearly, in the home. My wife and I are the parents of ten children, five sons and five daughters. All five sons and one daughter have served on missions. All six married children were married in the temple. Obviously there are other families that have done just as well, but it happens that recently a priesthood leader asked us to have our children put in writing their personal recollection of those things in our family's lifestyle that instilled within them their commitment to the gospel. Their responses reveal several things of significance, one of which is the overwhelming influence of the mother in the development of children's character and spiritual capacity. Another factor was that there was a consistency throughout all of the family's activity of seeking after those things that are "virtuous, lovely, of good report, or praiseworthy."

Following are some excerpts from the responses:

"We knew the Sabbath day was a holy day. That meant we could go to Church and have a special family dinner. We could write brothers or sisters on missions. We could never play with friends. We could never jump on the trampoline or watch television or go shopping. After moving to Utah, we would go to the Tabernacle Choir broadcast on Sunday mornings when we had Church at a later hour. Basically, Sunday was a family day."

"We always had to be reverent during sacrament meetings. We were expected to sit quietly, sing the hymns, and think, at least until after the sacrament. When we were little we could then be allowed to look at appropriate books or draw pictures."

"We always had family prayer . . . every day. When we were small, Mom would always kneel beside our beds and listen to our personal prayers, especially when we didn't want to say our prayers."

"We always had scripture study. One year when Mom was teaching at a private Christian school in Salt Lake, which was about a thirty-minute drive from home, she insisted that we six children who were attending the school she taught at read aloud from the Book of Mormon on the way to school. We each had our own copy, which we kept in the car, and by the end of the year, we had read the entire Book of Mormon out loud, on the way to school."

"We had a weekly family council to 'touch base' and to plan transportation and financial needs. We wrote down important family events and upcoming games, concerts, speaking assignments, etc. on a family calendar."

"We always sang together. We learned the hymns and Primary

songs. When we were in the car, we would take turns choosing our favorite songs or rounds, and we would sing together. Everyone was expected to learn a musical instrument and was expected to practice every day. Mom did not allow rock music in the house. She often had classical music on the stereo or on the FM radio. She was always taking us to concerts."

"We had a family library. Mom was always reading new books before she would let us read them, to determine whether they were appropriate. She would always have two or three new books for us to read, and she kept book charts in the kitchen. When we had read a certain number of books we qualified for a special treat . . . an afternoon in the park, dinner at a special restaurant, going to a special concert, etc."

"Everything was a learning experience, even vacations. When we took a trip, we read about where we were going. We visited museums. We never had time just to 'hang out.' We were always doing something. I thought every family did things together, but I was amazed when I got older to discover that a lot of my friends never did things like visit art galleries or museums with their families. They never visited the Church History Museum. Anytime friends would visit us, we would go to the This Is the Place Monument, or Temple Square, or the museums."

"One thing our parents always tried to do was say something positive about sacrament meeting, to involve the children in a discussion about what they learned from the speakers, how they felt during the beautiful music, and what message they thought Heavenly Father wanted them to remember. We never, never, never heard our parents criticize Church leaders or Church speakers."

"We were aware that Mom and Dad frequently went to the temple together. They never said much about it, but we knew it was something very important to them. When we lived in California we knew that they had to drive two or three hours just to get to the temple, so it must have been awfully important to them."

"We were always taught how to and expected to do work around the home. Mom expected all of the children to do their own laundry when they turned ten years old (she said that then we would be experts when we went on missions or away to college)."

One last word about family scripture study. One son commented: "Now I know that it was a real struggle for you and Dad to get us all up for scripture study in the mornings before school, because none of us children was very cooperative. We wanted to sleep in one more hour before school. I remember scripture study when one child would be sleeping on the couch, another would be face down on the floor, and others would be slumped in their seats. Yet you and Dad always had us read several verses and help the little ones who couldn't repeat their scripture verses. Now, none of us miss the sleep we wanted then. But we all remember that scripture study was a very important part of our family life, and that we never went to school without reading the scriptures."

Let me change the subject from inside the home to our responsibility to be "in the world" even though we will not partake of the ways of the world. The Latter-day Saints have a mission to fulfill in providing their support to the many honorable people who are struggling to carry on the fight against pornography. In the *Ensign* magazine of May, 1978, the First Presidency of the Church reaffirmed the counsel to members of the Church to be actively involved in their community, more especially in dealing with issues that have an effect upon the moral climate of the community. Among other things they said: "We urge our members to do their civic duty and to assume their responsibilities as individual citizens in seeking solutions to the problems which beset our cities and communities. . . . Church members cannot ignore the many practical problems that require solution if our families are to live in an environment conducive to spirituality. Where solutions to these practical problems require cooperative action with those not of our faith, members should not be reticent in doing their part in joining and leading in those efforts where they can make an individual contribution to those causes which are consistent with the standards of the Church" (*Ensign,* May, 1978, p. 100).

This urging of the First Presidency's continues a long-standing policy of the Church that is in harmony with the revelation to Joseph Smith recorded in Section 58 of the Doctrine and Covenants: "For behold, it is not meet that I should command in all things. . . . Verily I say, men should be anxiously engaged in a good cause, and do many things of their own free will, and bring to pass much righteousness; for the power is in them, wherein they are agents unto themselves" (D&C 58:26–28).

The presence of pornography in our society must be opposed whenever it appears and wherever it appears. Across the United States there are numerous organizations of honorable citizens who are determined to maintain standards of decency in their communities that will be conducive to living in a righteous society. It is my personal opinion that the members of The Church of Jesus Christ of Latter-day Saints are not doing anywhere near as much as they could be doing to lend strength and support to these organizations. In my travels and association with these people I find that there are seldom members of the Church laboring with them for the cause of truth and virtue.

Whether the issue be pornography in an adult bookstore, pornographic materials being sold from local "convenience" stores, pornography on cable TV, pornography on the Internet, or whatever other medium the pornographers may choose to use, we must not only oppose them but must also continue the fight until they are defeated and forced to abandon their evil enterprises. Prophets of the past have warned us of the consequences if the land continues to ripen in iniquity: "And [Alma] said: Thus saith the Lord God— Cursed shall be the land, yea, this land, unto every nation, kindred, tongue, and people, unto destruction, which do wickedly, when they are fully ripe; and as I have said so shall it be; for this is the cursing and the blessing of God upon the land, for the Lord cannot look upon sin with the least degree of allowance" (Alma 45:16).

The prophet Moroni was given a vision of our day, the day in which the Book of Mormon would come forth. He saw our nation, our lifestyles, our spiritual pollutions upon the land, and in a prophetic warning to us whom he saw in vision he said: "Behold, the sword of vengeance hangeth over you; and the time soon cometh that he avengeth the blood of the saints upon you, for he will not suffer their cries any longer" (Mormon 8:41).

Perhaps most powerfully Moroni, as he was abridging the record of the Jaredites, learned that they had been destroyed by secret combinations, as had his own people. As a military commander he had seen the evil combinations destroy his own civilization. As a seer and revelator he read from the twenty-four gold plates that such combinations had destroyed the Jaredites. As a prophet speaking to our generation he saw in vision our day and the emergence of evil combinations whose mission is to destroy our society. In the most solemn terms he prophecied of our ultimate destruction if we allow these secret combinations to continue their conspiracy of evil against our freedom. So he wrote:

> And now, we can behold the decrees of God concerning this land, that it is a land of promise; and whatsoever nation shall possess it shall serve God, or they shall be swept off when the fulness of his wrath shall come upon them. And the fulness of his wrath cometh upon them when they are ripened in iniquity.
>
> For behold, this is a land which is choice above all other lands; wherefore he that doth possess it shall serve God or shall be swept off. . . .
>
> And this cometh unto you, O ye Gentiles, that ye may know the decrees of God—that ye may repent, and not continue in your iniquities until the fulness come, that ye may not bring down the fulness of the wrath of God upon you as the inhabitants of the land have hitherto done. (2 Ether 9–11)

> And whatsoever nation shall uphold such secret combinations, to get power and gain, until they shall spread over the nation, behold, they shall be destroyed. . . .
>
> Wherefore, O ye Gentiles, it is wisdom in God that these things should be shown unto you, that thereby ye may repent of your sins, and suffer not that these murderous combinations shall get above you, which are built up to get power and gain. (Ether 8:22–23)

It seems to me that these secret combinations of evil and conspiring people of whom I have written herein receive far too much financial support and thereby personal approval from Latter-day Saints. Many of us pay our money to see their motion pictures and their videocassettes, to buy and listen to their obscene music, to wear their fashionable clothing; many subscribe to and read their slick magazines and accept far too much of the propaganda for evil that they contain; and in other ways many of us approve and extol their efforts to destroy our freedom through the destruction of our righteousness.

While he was President of the Church, John Taylor gave a very clear and unequivocal mandate to the Latter-day Saints regarding their "duty" to exercise all of their capacity to protect their families and their communities from the powers of evil. Said he: "God will have a free people, and while we have a duty to perform to preach the gospel, we have another to perform, that is, to stand up in the defense of human rights—in the defense of our own rights, the rights of our children, and in defense of the rights of this nation and of all men, no matter who they may be, and God being our helper to maintain those principles and to lift up a standard for the honorable of this and other nations to flock to, that they may be free from the tyranny and oppression that is sought to be crowded upon them. This is the duty we have to perform, and in the name of Israel's God we will do it" (*Journal of Discourses*, 23:239).

President Taylor recognized the relationship between loss of moral values, especially among those who are in positions of civic trust, and the ultimate triumph of evil. He warned that the destiny of those people who allow evil persons and evil principles to ascend would be to "become as wicked as Sodom." Said President Taylor: "Certainly if any person ought to interfere in political matters, it should be those whose minds and judgments are influenced by correct principles—religious as well as political. Otherwise those persons professing religion would have to be governed by those who make no professions; be subject to their rule; have the law and word of God trampled under foot, and become as wicked as Sodom. . . . The cause of humanity, the cause of justice, the cause of freedom, the cause of patriotism, and the cause of God requires us to use our endeavors to put in righteous rulers. Our revelations tell us to *seek diligently* for good and wise men" (*The Gospel Kingdom,* [Salt Lake City: Bookcraft, 1987], pp.320-321).

We are told that one of the signs of the "last days" will be "that every man that will not take his sword against his neighbor must needs flee unto Zion for safety." Further, the inhabitants of Zion "shall be the only people that shall not be at war one with another" (D&C 45:68–69). That state of virtual anarchy and violence is exactly what happened to the Nephites when evil became so prevalent among them that the "light of Christ" could no longer remain in their souls. This is when they became so filled with corruption that they were "past feeling."

This is also the exact result in the individual life that comes from the consumption of pornography. This is what allows the hideous conduct toward other human beings that we have noted earlier—the rape, the torture, the ultimate taking of human life, even of defenseless children, by those whose appetite for pornography has left them completely as the lowest form of "natural man," an enemy to God.

If we do not do something more than we are doing now, the prophetic warning given above will become the fate of our nation. The Internet and the videocassette bring the darkest, most vile of behavior into the life of any who will accept it. Their ultimate destiny will be the loss of all sense of decency and humanity. That is when stability in the community maintained by obedience to law will end, and each man will have to defend his home and family against the conduct of those too evil to be restrained in any other way. This is what happened to the Nephites and the Jaredites as they allowed secret combinations to get above them, and it is what will happen to any society that tolerates the presence of these secret combinations and their ability to extol evil, carnality, and violence.

It is of these circumstances that Moroni stated to our generation, "Wherefore, the Lord commandeth you, when ye shall see these things come among you that ye shall awake to a sense of your awful situation, because of this secret combination, which shall be among you. . . . For it cometh to pass that whoso buildeth it up seeketh to overthrow the freedom of all lands, nations, and countries; and it bringeth to pass the destruction of all people, for it is built up by the devil" (Ether 8:24–25).

And finally we have Moroni's notation about the ultimate cause of the destruction of both his own people and the Jaredites: "For so great had been the spreading of this wicked and secret society that it had corrupted the hearts of all the people" (Ether 9:6).

On the many occasions that I was in the presence of those who defended the pornographers, the representatives of the motion picture industry, the publishers of the slick magazines, the attorneys of the ACLU and their ilk, I soon learned to recognize a very powerful sensation of evil, of the "mists of darkness" that enveloped all that they said and did. I have a very literal and unequivocal witness of the Spirit that these are among those of the "secret combinations" of whom the Lord warned us through his prophet Moroni and the living prophets of our own dispensation. I have seen their duplicity, their absolute contempt for virtue and purity, their total lust for money and power. They are they who are the literal servants of Satan in what is perhaps his last great effort to defeat the Christ.

We have no excuse for further vacillation. There is no longer any justification for the attitude of "neutrality" in the face of this threat to our survival as a Church and a people of God. When we sit in a motion picture theater and do not even recognize the fact that the ideas and attitudes being presented (easily camouflaged as humor or drama) are inspired of Satan for the precise purpose of destroying our souls, then it is much later than we think.

As Alexander Pope so precisely noted,

> Vice is a monster of so frightful mien,
> As to be hated needs but to be seen;
> Yet seen too oft, familiar with her face,
> We first endure, then pity, then embrace.

Thus it would be well for each of us to re-examine our own tolerance of vice in the media that so totally surrounds us. First we need to affirm in our own mental attitudes our allegiance to "truth and virtue." Then within our homes, among our family members, we should make certain that we have taught our children to understand how subtle and deceitful the work of Satan has now become. Parents must be conscious of what their children see and hear—on the Internet, in the lyrics of the music they allow to enter their minds and hearts, and in the motion pictures in the theater and on videocassette in their homes.

Finally, we must no longer passively wait for others to contend with these secret combinations that are seeking to destroy us. If ever there was a time when we need faithful men and women to come forth and "wield the sword of justice in defense of truth and virtue," now is that time. In our communities, in the courts, in the legislative and congressional chambers, we must be present literally and figuratively, as Captain Moroni was when he wrote on the title of liberty: "In memory of our God, our religion, and freedom, and our peace, our wives and our children" (Alma 46:12).

In our day, Hugh Nibley has written: "There comes a time when the general defilement of a society becomes so great that the rising generation is put under undue pressure and cannot be said to have a fair choice between the way of light and the way of darkness. When such a point is reached, the cup of iniquity is full, and the established order that has passed the point of no return and neither can nor will change its ways must be removed physically and forcibly if necessary from the earth, whether by war, plague, famine, or upheavals of nature" (*An Approach to the Book of Mormon: The Collected Works of Hugh Nibley* [Salt Lake City: Deseret Book Company, 1985], 6:140).

May we, through efforts that seek to turn the tide, confidently join with Rudyard Kipling in his plea:

> "Judge of the nations, spare us yet,
> Lest we forget, lest we forget."

INDEX